A Chardonnay a Day

Vignettes That Bring Cheer

Enjoy every sip!
Maggie

MAGGIE MCCANN PIKE

Willow Creek Publications, LLC

Copyright © 2015 Maggie McCann Pike

All rights reserved. This book or any portion thereof may not be reproduced or used in any manner whatsoever without the express written permission of the publisher, except for the use of brief quotations in a book review.

Printed in the United States of America
First Printing, 2015

ISBN 978-0-9964611-0-8

Willow Creek Publications, LLC

www.maggiemccannpike.com

Table of Contents

A Note to the Reader • i
A Chardonnay a Day • iii

First Glass: **MELLOW**

    Mellow • 1
    Healing Colorado • 3
    Funeral Crashers • 7
    Identity Hijacked • 11
    Bookend Friendships • 15
    Hospice: How Can You Do It? • 19
    There's No Accounting for Perspective • 21
    I. Love. Teenagers. • 25
    Born to Love • 29
    Precious Little Black Thing • 31
    Lessons of Dementia • 33
    Vanished Memories • 37

Second Glass: **BUBBLY**

    Bubbly • 43
    The Legend of James and James in St. James • 45
    Identity Crisis • 49
    Vigilante • 53
    Abysmal Anosmia • 57
    Gawky Prom Date • 61
    Teenage Drama • 65
    Hotel Problematic • 69
    Roosters and Honey Buckets • 75
    My Secret Recipe • 79
    Inside Jokes • 83
    Jet Setter • 87

Third Glass: **UNDERAGED**
    Underaged • 93
    Bartley • 95
    Flash Mobs for Safety • 97
    Solomon Sarasin-Siskaroy • 99
    Misunderstood • 101
    Bartley Again • 105
    Loaves and Fishes • 107
    The Burden of Boots • 109
    The Day My Family Moved—Without Me • 111
    Pagan Babies • 115
    Falsely Accused • 119
    Bartley Barges into Adolescence • 123
    Freaked Out by Confirmation • 125
    Impoverished on Goodrich • 129

Fourth Glass: **PUNGENT**
    Pungent • 135
    Djangoed • 137
    Granny • 139
    Sit at the Cat's Table • 143
    Splash Party • 145
    Driver's License Angst • 149
    Pleasure Reading for the Common Good • 151
    Kidnapped: Caring Enough • 153
    Those Teachers Are At It Again • 157
    Sweet Justice without Violence • 159
    Showdown in the Showroom • 161

Fifth Glass: **BLUSH**
    Blush • 171
    Trapped at Water World • 173
    Mountain Biking Debacle • 175
    Blunder • 177

Crappy Diem • 181
Altar of the Lord • 183
Seeking a Bit o' Fiber • 185
The Secret Life of Jeans • 189
Redeemed • 193
Busted • 195
Good Chemistry • 197
Historic Error • 201
Dance at Zero Dark Thirty • 205

A Note to the Reader

Out of respect for the subjects in this book, I have disguised some minor details (including names when necessary), particularly in sensitive cases. Of course, I have written the subjects' stories with their full permission, but be advised that a few—especially when we get to people's most embarrassing moments—may contain a scintilla of extrapolation, a soupçon of speculation, or a hint of hyperbole where the memory, either mine or my subject's, failed.

I blame it on the Chardonnay.

A Chardonnay a Day

"The air is wine."
—Jack London, *John Barleycorn*

Before you dash for the corkscrew, let me clarify: this is not a book about wine.

It *is* wine.

It's a tasting of tales, a generous pouring of my own experiences, perspectives, and musings meant to entice you to sit back and mull things over, maybe even chuckle occasionally, as if wine were taking its effect on you.

In the same spirit that Jack London was moved to exclaim, "The air is wine," while loping across Sonoma Mountain atop his steed, I seek to lift your mood as fermented grapes do.

One story at a time.

A Chardonnay a day.

Follow me in your imagination to the vineyards of Sonoma and Napa Valleys, where there is something for everyone.

Vine-covered stone wineries with their pointed roofs and small, arched windows and doors welcome casual tasters and connoisseurs alike into their seductive embrace. But it's the bouquet, body, and balance of the distilled potions that keep them there. Bliss for a wine lover's palate.

For the painter's palette, equally appealing. Rows of grapevines wind around verdant hills and stretch to the horizon in perfect perspective, bursting with vigorous Chardonnay fruits. Robust rosebushes at the end of each row add to the beauty but also help the winemaker gauge the health of the crop. Hot air balloons sweep across the sky, smooth and bulbous like the grapes on the vines below.

It's intoxicating without so much as a sip.

Even the literature lover has a reason to worship wine country: Jack London lived there. Simply in need of some mellow time, he built his dream house near Glen Ellen in Sonoma. His later writings reflected his love of the simple pleasures of country life, and that perfect setting prompted him to write this reflection:

> I ride over my beautiful ranch. Between my legs is a beautiful horse. The air is wine. The grapes on a score of rolling hills are red with autumn flame. Across Sonoma Mountain, wisps of sea fog are stealing. The afternoon sun smolders in the drowsy sky. I have everything to make me glad I am alive.

In fact, at the Jack London Museum on the site of his home, the sign states that he wrote for one reason only: to earn enough money to make improvements on his property. Between books, he dabbled in scientific agriculture, researching ways to prolong the health of the land rather than exploit it, as earlier settlers had. He and his wife, Charmian, invested $80,000 in their dream mansion, Wolf House, and supervised its construction. But tragically, shortly before its completion, it burned down. Modern forensic experts blame spontaneous combustion, but at the time, Jack and Charmian feared an unknown enemy had deliberately set the fire. Fortunately, the Londons still had their small, wood-frame ranch house on the property, so Jack built a study where he could write, surrounded by his crops and the great outdoors.

As a reader and writer, I can lose myself in a mental picture of Jack and Charmian outside the windowed home, shaded by trees on Beauty Ranch, relaxing with a Chardonnay, chunks of cheese, and a clump of sumptuous grapes, waxing philosophical about their losses and joys. I imagine their sighs of gratitude for the thousand acres they had accrued, blended with regret over their aborted around-the-world sailing adventure. They surely celebrated Jack's writing success while grieving his immensely painful kidney condition. I would guess they laughed at the foibles of human nature, even as they cried over the trials life posed.

Such is the real world that London sought to be a part of, a world marked by a sinuous path that often defied the order he tried to give it. Yet by all accounts, he embraced it with boundless enthusiasm.

And I invite you to do the same.

Come to my metaphorical wine gathering. Grab a goblet from the server's tray. Sip the enchanting elixir, chill with friends, and stay until the brilliant orange sun glistens through your glass on its way to bed.

This collection of personal essays is divided into five sections, each with a name that embodies the character of the stories it contains, using the same descriptive terms you would find on a wine bottle. It is my hope that as you read them, you'll actually feel the Chardonnay course through your body.

The first glass finds us mellow, not yet intoxicated, just basking in the tender aura of good company and fine wine. The second glass brings a lighthearted, bubbly feeling. With the third glass, we start reminiscing, and stories about our children and our own childhoods lighten the mood. By the fourth, the guests have all imbibed, and loose-lipped tales and opinions dart through the air, some just sober, some downright pungent. With the fifth drink, the whole lot of us are making fools of ourselves, pure and simple.

All this without a drop of alcohol touching your lips. After all, even Jack London, in his autobiographical novel, *John Barleycorn*, cautioned against overindulging, based on his own regrets.

No, you'll not use wine to have a good time.

The written word will be your Chardonnay.

So start sipping. Immerse yourself in these vignettes, a blend of memories, reflections, opinions, woolgathering, and embarrassing moments.

Here, indeed, the air is wine.

First Glass
MELLOW

Mellow

A mellow wine: one that has a full and pleasing flavor through proper aging.

A mellow person: one who has attained to kindliness or gentleness through age and experience.

A mellow life: one that's unhurried and relaxed.

Sign me up.

There was a time when my life was about as unhurried and relaxed as a tsunami. Every path I followed seemed designed to stretch me to my limits. I was bound to duty. The clock became my corset, the computer my handcuffs, my car an onerous appendage.

I remember the day I attended a talk at a retreat center on the outskirts of town. I'd left home late, fought traffic all the way, and screeched into the parking lot, practically on two wheels, with barely a minute to spare. I tore up the sidewalk to the door, flew into the conference room, and jolted the chairs on either side of me as I plopped down to listen.

This is how I arrived everywhere I went.

Quiet reflection time was no more serene. *Speed walk around the grounds*, I told myself. *It's good for your metabolism.*

What I really needed, but didn't know it, was a hammock. I needed repose.

Then one day, after years of darting about here and there at the speed of a sailfish, I found myself pulling into the parking lot of that same retreat center, that same stately, spired chapel this time inviting me to come inside, slow down, and rest awhile.

And as I rounded the small hill that brought the soaring Rocky Mountains into full view, I noticed something else. Where that majestic backdrop met the edge of the retreat center lawn was a sight I would have never expected.

A cow.

Clearly, it was a sign from the Divine. Of this I was sure, because at that very moment, wisps of a poem by Welsh writer W.H. Davies breezed into my head, as gently and kindly as a dove:

MAGGIE McCANN PIKE

> What is this life if, full of care,
> We have no time to stand and stare?
> No time to stand beneath the boughs,
> And stare as long as sheep and cows.

Concluding with:

> A poor life this if, full of care,
> We have no time to stand and stare.

And that was that. Something shifted within.

Age and experience followed, bringing more moments of meditation and contemplation that once, as a tired and frenetic mom and employee, I had no time for.

But now, I take in all the layers of life, savoring each of their full and pleasing flavors.

I've mellowed.

Tom Hodgkinson, editor of *The Idler* and proponent of a relaxed approach to life advises: "Find a culture where loafing is the order of the day and where they don't understand our need to be constantly doing things. Find somewhere you can have a hammock holiday."

Indeed. Live mellow.

Healing Colorado

This vignette was published as a guest commentary in the Denver Post *on July 22, 2012*

Rain. If only.

Pain. Leave us alone.

My daughter Betsy and I craved respite from the hottest summer on record in Colorado, suffocating heat that dared to slither from June into July, and then into August. One fire after another, fueled by strong winds, had scorched our parched land, burned our dream homes, and ushered smoke into our three-hundred-days-a-year azure skies.

The most destructive fire season in state history, they said.

Oh, if only rain.

And then deranged tragedy dug its evil claws even deeper into our damaged souls. A gunman massacred twelve theatergoers and injured fifty-eight more in the suburb next door, Aurora, Colorado.

One of the deadliest mass shootings in U.S. history, they said.

Terror reigned in its aftermath. Now even the cinema, our traditional go-to for relaxation and entertainment, wasn't safe.

Pain, just go away.

"We gotta get outta here," implored my daughter, a tinge of panic in her voice.

"But where can we go?" I moaned. Wisps and plumes and billows from the north, the south, and the west were still holding us captive.

Then, at last, the infernos called a ceasefire. Our firefighter heroes had beaten the life out of them and set Colorado free.

Betsy and I tiptoed out of the devastation and peeked again at a map.

"Pagosa Springs, maybe? Let's give it a try." And off we went.

It took us mere miles to realize that where Mother Nature had thrown a tantrum, Colorado, calm and reliable, had triumphed. The splendor we had always known our state to hold lay before us in full force.

The pristine expanse of South Park as we made our descent on Highway 285.

Charming Salida, its Riverside Park cradling us in its stately trees as the Arkansas River swirled in currents inches away from the young waders.

The dramatic sentinel of sheer cliffs and pine spires that line Wolf Creek Pass.

A side trip to the mystical Great Sand Dunes.

And at last, Pagosa Springs. It was the Ute Indians who had named the place "Pah gosah," meaning "healing waters." If we couldn't have rain, and had to have pain, then the eighteen tiered pools bubbling with natural mineral waters above the San Juan River would help.

We basked in the tranquility of it all. For hours.

Late afternoon found us sitting on the outdoor terrace of Tequila's Restaurant directly across from the hot springs, large umbrellas protecting us from the brilliant sun. Below, the river, pregnant with tubers, steered children down its canal in the coolness of its nurturing waters.

Then, without warning, the sky took on a somber hue. An enormous, dark cloud rumbled across the heavens and took its place above us. With a loud crack, the cloud split open and poured its contents, like a gigantic egg from the top of the beanstalk, onto the earth below. It was a torrential monsoon, not a common sight in Colorado.

Waiters scrambled to our area, urging us to head inside. Two parents with a baby gathered their things and raced for cover. Three other tables evacuated posthaste, and huddled together under the protection of the roof.

But Betsy and I stayed. The umbrella was our protector, the raindrops that touched us, minimal. We savored the cool rain that filled our every arid cell with the waters of life. The true healing waters.

A deep voice behind us pierced the silence. "Hey, you two! We're the only ones to stay. You're troopers! I LOVE you!" An earthy man with a ponytail and undying exuberance turned toward us from the next table. He got up and did a little dance in the rain.

His wife joined him. "We just survived the Waldo Canyon fire. We were evacuated and thought for sure we were going to lose our house."

"Come on, rain!" shouted our new friends.

"Bring it!" screamed Betsy and I.

We dove into their fun, volleying quips back and forth. The force of the downfall increased until we felt the sheets of water finally tumbling off the umbrella and into our faces.

But we stayed, all four of us.

Pure glee bonded strangers that afternoon on the terrace above Pagosa Springs.

Yes, Colorado had suffered horrendous devastation, and heartache for those of us who care about each other.

But life springs eternal and nowhere was it more evident than here in our state.

Perhaps the best way to heal Colorado is to get out there and soak in all that beauty.

Funeral Crashers

We honestly never intended to crash a funeral.

It was a Monday afternoon and my friend Kathy and I were driving east on Interstate 70 from Beaver Creek, Colorado, back to Denver. As we approached stunning Vail Valley, the lush, green slopes, dramatic rock formations, and charming European décor of the village screamed, "Come visit!"

At that moment, I remembered that Vail gave free gondola rides during the off-season, and the very thought of viewing Vail from above had me drooling. With a sudden jerk of the wheel, I exited into the town before I even had a chance to ask my friend if she would like to take this adventure with me. I flung open the car door and pushed Kathy to the waiting line.

"I don't really like heights—" She had barely uttered the words when a sudden jolt and a startling *whoosh* signaled our ascent into the heavens above Vail, Colorado.

As we all took our seats to enjoy the ride, someone handed out fliers. The man whose face was profiled on the leaflet was quite handsome, so I figured he was either a real-estate agent or the next aspiring mayor of Vail. I tucked the paper into my jeans pocket.

As expected, the view was breathtaking. For me, this meant I was emotionally moved; for Kathy, it meant she really couldn't breathe. Her ashen face matched her white knuckles gripping the bar, but to her credit, she politely ooh-ed and ahh-ed on cue. Despite the spectacular vistas, I was surprised at how quiet everybody else was. *Oh well*, thought I. *Apparently the dazzling panorama has left everyone speechless. It happens.*

Twenty minutes later, we debarked from the gondola. A few people bearing warm smiles offered all the passengers hot chocolate and lemonade, which I accepted with slight confusion. I knew for sure I'd never received free hot chocolate at the top of Vail Mountain.

Before hopping back on for the ride down, we thought we'd take a short hike and see what we could see. We followed the crowd, ending up in what appeared to be an outdoor theater, complete with rows of folding chairs and a large screen. People were mingling, like neighbors at an ice cream social. It was clear we had walked right into a party. *Oops.*

"Psst," I whispered to my friend. "I think we're—maybe—not supposed to be here."

"Okay," she answered, a little too quickly. "Let's go." I admit, she did still look a little ghostly.

"Wait a sec. Let's go inside that building till we figure out what this is," I suggested. I dragged my comrade up some stairs to a window that overlooked the revelry below. A well-dressed man was standing next to me, reading the same flier we had received on the way up.

"Excuse me," I interrupted. "Do you know what this event is?"

"It's a funeral," he said. "Dan died three months ago. He wanted his ashes scattered on Vail Mountain, so we're having a memorial service."

Gulp. "Kathy," I implored in hushed tones. "We're at Dan's funeral. Hurry! Let's read the flier." I dug the paper out of my jeans pocket.

We read how this much-loved man, only forty-two years old and a member of the ski patrol, had died suddenly in March, in the place he loved as home. He had left a bereaved wife and countless friends in the Vail community.

"How did we end up at a funeral?" I muttered out of the side of my mouth.

"I don't know, but we have to slip out of here gracefully," Kathy answered.

That wasn't as easy as it sounded. Even on the sidelines of Dan's funeral, mourners came and went, meeting our eyes with compassion, as we did theirs.

We couldn't just bolt. That would be heartless.

"Hello," I said to a woman clad in fashionable mountain wear, who clearly shared Dan's love of the outdoors. "He really lived life to the fullest, didn't he? How many of us can say we died doing what we love most?"

"Yes, yes he did. He was a great friend," she said.

And to the elderly gentleman whose ruddy complexion indicated he may have served on the ski patrol, perhaps as Dan's boss, I commented, "It sounds like Dan was a dedicated worker. Twenty years on the job—wow!"

"Yup. They don't make 'em like that anymore," he concurred.

I even managed to grab someone who looked like she knew everyone and asked, "Do you know which one is Dan's wife?" The lady pointed to a petite woman, young and vibrant, who was chatting animatedly with a guest.

"Oh, bless her heart," I sympathized. "So young to be a widow."

In the meantime, my fellow interloper, now adjusted to the altitude, had suddenly come to life and was having her own conversations, bestowing compassion right and left onto Dan's friends. Between us, we peppered the dialogue with every funeral platitude we had ever heard.

To one: "I wish there were words to comfort you."

To another: "I'm shocked and saddened by your loss."

"He was such a fine person."

"What you're going through must be very difficult."

"He lived a full life and was an inspiration to everyone."

At the end of the ceremony, Kathy and I walked slowly toward the gondola for our return trip. Come to find out, the gondola was normally closed on Mondays, and was only open that day to transport mourners to Dan's funeral.

The serendipity did not elude us. Once you accidentally find yourself at a funeral, you sort of have to join in the grieving. The irony at the top of Vail Mountain was that once we had celebrated Dan's life with his family and friends, our shared loss was sincere.

Identity Hijacked

The cryptic text message gave me the chills:

> You read tarot cards? One more thing I didn't know about you.

I texted back:

> What?! This is Maggie. Did you text the wrong person?

And the reply, even more cryptic:

> No, it's you. Talking to a man named Benjamin over here at Coffee Perks. Said you read his cards. Got your name from his mom, who's a friend of yours.

Oh no, here we go again.

I've never faced the horror of having my identity stolen, at least not for nefarious reasons. But someone who shares my name has been making mischief in my life for quite some time.

The whole bizarre story started in 1990 when my busybody neighbor, Nancy, stopped by to visit. Her opener, dripping with sympathy, was, "How are you doing? Is there anything I can pray for?"

I knew Nancy well. She always disguised her gossip with the words, "Pray for so-and-so because . . ." before launching into the graphic details of so-and-so's scandal.

But this time, apparently, *I* was the subject of scandal, so I heard her out.

I was soon distracted from our conversation by her frequent glances around the kitchen where we sat. When she got a little too close and appeared to be sniffing around my face, I finally stopped her.

"What is it you're looking for, for heaven's sake?"

"Well," Nancy explained. "I saw your item in the church bulletin last Sunday inviting parishioners to an Alcoholics Anonymous meeting that you're getting started."

I had no idea how to respond.

"I never knew that about you, so I wanted to let you know that I'm there for you, one day at a time."

"Nancy, that wasn't me. You've known me for years. I don't drink."

"But it was your name in the bulletin," she argued.

Finally, Nancy left. Twenty minutes later, my phone rang. It was Nancy.

"I have the bulletin right here in front of me," she said. "Now I find out you're not only starting the AA support group, but you're trying to get a pinochle group going at church."

Oh, geez.

And that was the first time my name-alike walked into my life.

Fast forward five years. I was applying for teaching jobs now that all five of my children were in school. I got a callback interview from a nearby school district, and my heart soared with hope. In I walked. The interviewer thumbed through my folder.

"Hmm," he said. "The notation on your application indicates we've already interviewed you."

"Well, yes. Isn't this a second interview?"

"No." Hope took a dive. "Oh wait—I have two applications with the same name. Did you send in two?"

There she was again. My namesake had applied to the same school district. My only thought: *I hope she has a good reputation. From now on, both our jobs are at stake.*

Fast forward three years. I was at my dermatologist's office getting my annual mole check. She perused my file and reported, "Well, good news. The cancer is under control. We'll keep an eye on it—"

I was shocked. "*Huh?* When did I get cancer?"

"The growth on . . . wait. Do I have the wrong file? Is this your address?"

It wasn't.

"I *thought* you didn't look familiar," she said. "You have the same name as another of my patients. I'll have to be more careful."

"Indeed," I muttered.

Fast forward another year.

I'd been away from my high school teaching job for a year, having taken a literacy position in an elementary school. One day my colleagues from the high school called me, chortling.

"We just had the funniest thing happen. We interviewed a woman with your same name. We thought it was you wanting to teach French again, so we were all set to have some fun interviewing you. The same name! What are the chances?"

Pretty good, apparently. Now we belong to the same parish, have the same doctor, apply for the same jobs, and teach the same subject.

Fast forward again.

The phone rang.

"This is Allstate Insurance calling about your accident claim."

My what?

"Uh, I wasn't in an accident."

"Oh, yes you were," she informed me, in that I've-heard-this-before tone of voice. "I'm referring to the head-on collision in southern Colorado last Friday. The one where you ran a red light at that intersection that crosses the highway."

"What are you talking about?" I gripped the life out of the phone. This was getting surreal. "My car was in my school's parking lot in Highlands Ranch. I wasn't in southern Colorado."

"Hmm. That's strange," said the claims adjuster. "It says here you were seriously injured and have been hospitalized. How are you feeling now?"

"I'm not in the hospital. I'm standing upright in my kitchen as I talk to you."

And now I'm reading tarot cards.

Really. *Really.* What *are* the chances?

Bookend Friendships

A version of this essay appeared in the February 2015 edition of Business Heroine Magazine *(businessheroinemagazine.com)*

We value friendship so much, we've created an entire holiday that revolves around love. Every Valentine's Day, from early childhood through old age, we think about who our best friends are and honor them with a token of our love. If we're lucky, some of the same little guys and girls who received our one-sided, heart-filled cards scrawled with "yur frend" in our best childhood penmanship, are still on our Valentine's list. After all, nineteenth-century Welsh composer Joseph Parry gave us true words of wisdom when he wrote, "Make new friends, but keep the old; those are silver, these are gold."

But it's rarely that simple. Much has been written about the seasons of friendships—the right person appearing when we need a friend, then both parties moving on after the friendship has run its course.

I've discovered a wonderful truth, however: some of those who played a significant role in our early lives, but have been long absent, now have an equally important part to play in later life.

I call these "bookend friendships"—friends at the beginning and end, with tomes of unshared life in between the bookends.

My own life has harbored a collection of friends, very few of whom have traveled with me from the beginning. Most have wandered into my life at various points, and while many did stay, others disappeared.

But for joy! Some reappeared.

And those are the magical, almost mystical, friendships. The richness of a bookend friendship lies in the powerful blend of those-are-silver and these-are-gold.

I've been blessed with a number of these treasures in my later years.

Gianeen, for example.

Fifty years ago, my best friend, Gianeen, and I had a horrible fight about whatever it is middle schoolers fight about, and she never spoke to me again. Left behind were just the first pages of our shared life—five short years of school, Brownie Scouts, secret clubs, roller skating, and neighborhood night games.

And then, thirty years later, a letter arrived.

From Gianeen.

She wondered where life had taken me, and assured me that she had thought of me on my birthday every year. After filling each other in on the chapters of our lives since we'd parted, we resumed our friendship, though from distant states. The kicker was when she asked, "Why was it we stopped being friends? I can't remember."

Recently, Gianeen came to my town for a brief visit. We stared into each other's faces, our eyes lined with wrinkles, but twinkling still. We walked into the house, a little more slowly than before, but with the pep of excitement. And we talked as if we'd never been apart.

Pure silver, pure gold.

In the course of our conversation we discovered we both shared the same bucket list item. So before she left for home, Gianeen and I went zip lining in the Rocky Mountains.

Our second bookend was now in place.

My reunion with Gianeen is only one of the bookends that flank the tomes of my life. I also reconnected with an elementary school teacher, several college friends who had faded away, and the most exhilarating of all: a slew of students I taught in the 1970s, three states away.

I was a mere twenty-two years old when I met those California high schoolers. Now we're practically the same age; what does ten years matter when you're this old? When I left their school, I thought I'd never see them again, and I wouldn't have but for Facebook, which led to a few visits to spend time with them in person. Volumes of their lives had unfolded during the long absence, every one of those "kids" outdoing me in one way or the other.

Purer silver, more precious gold I can't imagine.

All my friendships, these and those, hold value: the ones I've known steadily through many decades right along with the ones that survived a hiatus.

After all, as author Anaïs Nin wrote, "Each friend represents a world in us, a world possibly not born until they arrive, and it is only by this meeting that a new world is born."

The gift is in rediscovering what that original meeting was all about, and staying open to whatever new world might be born in the reconnection.

Hospice: How Can You Do It?

When I decided to become a hospice volunteer, it was because I wanted to tap something deeper in myself. I wasn't a complete stranger to the dying process. I had faced my dad's death with him, as well as the passing of my dear neighbor Mary, and of church friend Jane. And wow, what a powerful experience I shared with each of those who allowed me to spend time with them as they made their journeys. But I knew I had more to learn, and I craved it. So I signed up.

The best way I can describe hospice is as a model of care rather than a place. After all curative treatments have been exhausted, a patient chooses not to prolong death, but to allow it to happen in its own course, with pain control and dignity the main objectives. It seems so natural to me.

But from day one, I kept hearing the question that has now become routine: How can you do it?

The question comes most often from those who remember the unfathomable range of emotions they felt when their precious ones were dying. I don't know how *they* did it. Because my role is to visit with my patients and give respite to their caregivers, I'm there far less time than the family is, and in that way I don't feel the same intensity. Nor do I play the same role, or face the same challenges, as a nurse or chaplain would. I'm not there to *do*; I'm simply there to *be*.

So I can do it.

I can do it because when I'm with a patient, I don't feel like I'm with someone who is dying. I'm visiting someone who is very much alive. My patients are magnificent people engaged in this particular stage of their lives, and I find it a delight to be in their company.

Take Linda, for example, a sixty-six-year-old with a hearty laugh, a love of books, and an affinity for her TV idols, Rizzoli and Isles. Ordinary stuff.

The day she spewed a loud "Ish!" I knew I had a kindred spirit. As far as I know, only Minnesotans express disgust with the word "ish."

"When did you spend time in Minnesota?" I asked, surprising her. And we began yet another conversation about yet another branch of her rich life.

Another patient, Nellie, wore a crusty demeanor. Regarding her second husband, from whom she was separated, she said, "He's my best friend, but I can't live with him. Haven't lived with him in ten years." Yet within a month, both he and Nellie's ex-husband moved into her building to be near her.

I was apparently Nellie's preferred Scrabble partner. "This is my mental stimulation," she avowed, and yes, she beat my pants off every time. "I can't believe I trounced a writer," she gloated one day. It was not a pretty picture, Nell and I playing Scrabble.

And Aleksander. Aleksander was a distinguished-looking man who had played pro football when leather helmets were still part of the uniform. His tiny, ninety-two-year-old wife of seventy years was two years his senior. "Yes, I'm a cougar," she joked. Even though Aleksander slept a lot, my visits with his wife when she returned from her weekly garage sales kept me entertained. And did she have a mind of her own.

"I always serve Aleksander eggs, bacon, toast, fruit, cereal, and Ensure," she said. "Hospice told me not to force him to eat. What, are they trying to starve him to death?"

One day she told me how she handled his falls, this man a good eight inches taller than she: "Oh, I just push him up against the wall and run out into the cul-de-sac and yell till someone helps me."

I was actually with Aleksander when he died, which is not typical for a volunteer. But truly, it was as natural and peaceful as the hour I had just spent with him.

His lovely lady told me later how she had received the news. "Why, I just went ahead and had my nails done. I had an appointment. What else was I going to do?"

See? It's as normal as that.

That's why I'm a hospice volunteer.

And that's how I can do it.

There's No Accounting for Perspective

The Roman emperor Marcus Aurelius said, "Everything we see is a perspective, not the truth." In that respect, things haven't changed much since the first century AD. But I get a kick out of seeing what's important to people based on their takes on everyday phenomena.

For example, one advantage of having honeymooned with a geologist was learning about the spectacular rock formations that loom with majesty over our countryside. The ten-day road trip from St. Paul, Minnesota, to San Pedro, California, in August 1971 did not disappoint.

"Those faces were blasted out of granite," my new husband expounded at Mount Rushmore in South Dakota. "Granite rocks are igneous rocks formed by slowly cooling pockets of magma that were trapped beneath the earth's surface."

I never knew that. I never even knew I *wanted* to know that. I was busy noticing the makes and colors of cars on the highway, trying to imagine the life stories of the passengers inside.

"That's an alluvial fan," he coached me in several different western states, pointing out how water-transported material formed fan shapes at the bases of various slopes.

And at Bryce Canyon in Utah: "Bryce Canyon is carved by freeze-thaw cycles, not a river, so it's not really a canyon. Bryce is a Bryce."

My husband's earth-science perspective was contagious, and by the time we arrived in California, I was noticing geology everywhere, even though I hadn't mastered all the terms.

"Oh! Oh! I think I see an alluvial fan!" I shouted on our first day at the beach.

"No, just a sand dune," my science man corrected me.

This whole earth science thing was an eye opener for me because all my life, my siblings and I had been treated to botany and zoology lessons from our College of St. Thomas biology professor dad. Picnics, hikes, and Sunday drives to Uncle Clem's farm were the classroom where the McCann kids learned the workings of nature. Oak trees were distinctly different from elm and maple trees. Reptiles, amphibians, and all manner of insects were ours to inspect. Binoculars revealed the most extraordinary birds. So I had to make a shift to fit in with my husband's worldview.

When we moved from California to Colorado, my brother Doug, founder of the Sterling Fence Company in Minneapolis, came to visit. On an outing to view the beauty of this mountain state, we wandered past sparkling, turquoise lakes, jagged mountain peaks, and rolling, green valleys. The assault on the senses was unassailable.

Suddenly from the back seat of the car, Doug's voice sliced the solemn silence: "Wow! Look at those fences!"

Fences.

Not the mineral aggregates, not the lush foliage.

The fences.

It happens all the time. People tell us what's important to them with their casual comments. Mike notices only the tiling job at the quaint, charmingly decorated French café where we're dining. Roberto sees nothing but straight, white teeth amidst all the glitter of the Miss America pageant. The Carolina beaches are not enough for Mary without a visit to the mall, where she analyzes the efficacy of store displays. Sure enough: construction worker, dentist, retail executive. Each with a unique passion, each with a unique perspective.

There's no accounting for what we hold dear to us.

On the other side of the continent, in Washington, D.C., I was touring our nation's capital with my pilot son, Tim, and his flight attendant girlfriend. The powerful presence of history all around us was inspirational beyond words. The Washington Monument jutted upward and pierced the azure sky, while Lincoln and Jefferson gazed watchfully over D.C. from their respective sites. A glance down the street revealed the Capitol building, a thrilling sight for a tourist, but for the locals as ordinary as the McDonald's arches.

Later, as we approached the White House, I found myself absorbed in the awe-inspiring thought that right in front of me, presidents had lived and governed for over two hundred years, and had convened with leaders from all over the globe to determine the fate of the entire world.

Suddenly, my reverie was interrupted by an exuberant shriek. "Hey, check out that JetBlue A320 behind the monument!"

Apparently a plane was landing.

"Wow, that's awesome," added Tim. "I love that river approach."

"But what about the White House?" I felt compelled to ask.

In unison, the two glanced upward, off to the right, then upward again.

"You're right," Tim declared. "It does seem like it's flying a bit too close to the White House."

Not what I meant.

It's one of those crazy things, people's perspectives. Now, if we could just observe from each other's point of view, and add it to our own, we'd probably have a pretty accurate view of the world around us.

I. Love. Teenagers.

Teenagers are my idols. For countless reasons.

Case in point: A few years ago on a cold winter evening, my car's transaxle broke, which meant I couldn't shift gears. I had no choice but to drive the twelve miles home—cringe if you must—in first gear.

I couldn't take the freeway, so the snowy city streets played host to me in my distress. Hundreds of cars whizzed by until finally, I turned onto a quieter street. Soon, headlights appeared in my rear view mirror, so I pulled over to let the car pass. Instead, it stopped and five teenagers, girls and boys, piled out and ran toward me.

"Do you need some help?" they asked with obvious eagerness. "Can we give you a push? Need a ride somewhere? Should we call someone for you?"

I can't tell you how consoling it was to be wrapped in their blanket of caring. It wasn't the busy adults racing down Broadway. It was the teenagers.

In another incident, this time at the airport, I found myself in an exceedingly long line at the ticket counter, followed by a quadruple-snaked security queue. *That's it,* I moaned. *I'm not going to make my flight.*

Unless.

I tore to the head of the line, past a slew of disgusted faces, and immediately locked eyes with two young men in their late teens. Almost positive they would say yes, because that's how I knew teenagers to be, I asked if they would feel comfortable letting me go ahead of them in order to get to my plane on time. "Sure," they said without hesitation, as if I had just asked them if they liked pizza. They made my spirits soar.

My most recent reminder of the goodness of young people came in the music theory class I was taking at the community college, where I was surrounded by eighteen-year-olds, many of whom were already in rock bands and wanting to get some formal training in music fundamentals.

One of our classmates was a young man who bore the effects of shaken baby syndrome. Luke was extremely friendly and talkative, and had an unparalleled memory for the details of every rock group that ever existed. (Apparently I had a shirt exactly like one worn by Van Halen. Luke told me so.)

For Luke, music theory was difficult, because it's mathematical and takes a great deal of concentration. He needed time to process information. But extra processing time was a luxury in that class, and sadly, the instructor gave no indication that she was aware of Luke's differences.

"I'm really smart," he explained to me one day. "If she would just stop torturing me in front of the whole class, I think I could get it."

Everyone else knew he was different, though. He was eager to connect, but slightly awkward. Even though he'd talk to anyone that walked by, he spoke rapidly and barely made eye contact. Fortunately, no one in our class ever avoided him or showed unease.

So at our last session, Luke invited a couple of the guys to sit with him. I watched as they plopped down on either side of Luke, then listened as he showered the two head-shaven band members with music trivia. And I glowed inside seeing Luke receive nothing but respect from his two peers.

Fifteen minutes into class, the instructor asked Luke to clap and count the meter on page sixty-five.

"Oh, I'm sorry, I can't do that," stammered Luke. I could feel his panic as he looked at the wave of black dots and flags that swept over the page. They scared me, too.

"Well, try," she said.

Silence.

And then I heard a quiet, gentle voice next to Luke. "Dude, what number do you give the first note?"

"Oh, yeah. One," Luke ventured.

"Yeah. Now try 'one-and,' then go on to 'two-and,'" his seat partner prodded, lips barely moving.

Luke did.

Then the student on the other side of Luke joined in. "You got it, man," he whispered. "Just keep counting up to 'four-and,' then start over." He tapped his fingers on the table to guide Luke. And with that lift,

Luke got through all four measures.
> He looked up, beaming.
> His buddies looked down as if nothing had happened.
> I thought my heart was going to burst.

Born to Love

*This essay was published in the May 2015 edition
of* Business Heroine Magazine *(businessheroinemagazine.com)*

I have a confession. I *get* why Tom Hanks, playing a castaway, fell in love with his volleyball. After his airplane crashed in the South Pacific, Hanks's character, Chuck Noland, developed a deep attachment to Wilson, the volleyball he talked to, ribbed, and even argued with during the four years of his isolation. When Wilson was swept away into the ocean, Chuck's overwhelming sadness engulfed me, too. Where at first I rolled my eyes, by the end of the movie I was drowning in the same dark emptiness that Chuck felt.

I shouldn't have been surprised. It's in our nature to love.

I felt the same way the other day when I was driving from the southern suburbs of Denver, Colorado, into an area of downtown that was new for me. I had checked the directions online, visualized where I was going, jotted down my freeway exit, the lefts and the rights, the if-you-get-to-such-and-such-street-you've-gone-too-fars that would get me to my destination. I was all set.

But before I even left my driveway, unease began to fill me. Even if I didn't need a navigator, I wanted someone with me.

I grabbed Susie.

Susie's not typical of my usual BFF choices.

She's my GPS.

Susie's been on a few excursions with me. On a particularly long drive, a two-day trip from Denver to South Bend, Indiana, I drew comfort from Susie's lively, mechanical voice gently guiding me across the states. At times, I blush to say, I even let myself indulge in a guilty pleasure: with the push of a button, I changed Susie into Jacques-Pierre, the male French voice option. But mostly it was Susie who kept me company.

At one point, however, Susie became uncharacteristically quiet for several hours. I hadn't noticed at first, to tell the truth, but as the Iowa sun sank toward the west, dropping its filmy veil over the landscape, an air of sadness crept over me. I tapped the cold box, hoping to rouse my companion. *Talk to me, Susie. Say something, anything.* The words flitted into my mind faster than fireflies on the Iowa farmlands, and it took me by surprise. Where did such an insane notion come from, that Susie and I were really friends?

But is that any different from our first nonhuman love relationships: our blankets, our dollies, our pets? Or our later-in-life ones: The cheery tone of Mary Tyler Moore on TV—coveted adult companionship after hearing nothing but children's voices all day. The musician crooning in the background as we type in solitude. The framed photos in our workspaces that add humanity to our mundane tasks. Take them away, and it leaves a hole.

But nature abhors a vacuum, and when our heart yearns, it begs to be filled with connection. How amazing is it, whenever a relationship doesn't come in the form of a warm being, that our souls have the capacity to create bonds, even without reciprocation.

So volleyball, blanket, doll, pet, GPS. Cherish them all. Writes author Ellen J. Barrier: "Sharing the same passionate love with [another] gives a feeling of being alive! The experience of something real is unforgettable."

And so it is: we're born to love.

Precious Little Black Thing

I'm going to say up front that pet stories have always irritated me. I just never got it. I grew up with black labs: first Queenie, then Tar, but they were my dad's dogs for hunting, and they stayed outside. I had no heart for them whatsoever. I was always the one who would back away when a dog loped up and sniffed me with its wet snout. Yuck.

I could never have predicted that would change, but it did.

A number of years ago, my oldest daughter boomeranged briefly, bringing her black cocker spaniel into my home. Kalu (pronounced "COLL-oo") was so named because Anne had given him as a Christmas gift to her Nepalese beau, and in Nepal, "kalu" means something along the lines of "precious little black thing." Kalu spent his first year—a rather untamed one by all accounts—in Oakland, California, with Anne and her boyfriend. When the two parted ways, Anne came back to Denver with the dog. She soon found an apartment, except it had a no-pets policy, and when she asked if Kalu could stay with me, guess who wasn't tough enough to say no?

It wasn't that I didn't like Kalu. I liked him fine—from a distance. I had held him that Christmas Day eleven years ago when he was just a few inches long, and, against my will, I'd felt a confusing warmth in my heart.

It didn't help that Kalu was adorable even when Anne was buying him. She had initially chosen his smaller brother, but when she went to sign the papers, Kalu slapped his paw onto the page, demanding that she change her mind and adopt him instead. She did.

The tea party didn't help either. Anne had left Kalu at home in her Oakland apartment for a few hours, and when she returned, she couldn't believe what she saw. Kalu had placed his stuffed animals on the pillows that lay around the low table in the living room, and there he sat at the head of the table, entertaining his friends.

No, the reason I didn't want to have a dog is because I knew that one day I would lose him. And to invite that kind of pain into my life seemed insane.

But I did it anyway, and it has been the greatest gift a person could receive. I don't have to spell out to dog lovers all the joy I've known. And to those who are indifferent, as I once was, I won't bore you.

But I will say this: that bundle of love transformed me.

Today, Kalu's little body wouldn't hold on any longer, and he begged for relief from the cancer that filled him. Cradled by those of us who loved him, he slipped peacefully away at the hands of a caring veterinarian, on his favorite blanket in front of his favorite bay window, where the setting sun shimmered off his black coat and the maple leaves flickered like a dying flame.

In an instant, he was gone, and with him, his playful canter, our long walks, the snuggling. No more.

My heart was broken to pieces; the pain, indescribable.

Yet in the end, I think Alfred Lord Tennyson was right:

> I hold it true, whate'er befall;
> I feel it, when I sorrow most;
> 'Tis better to have loved and lost
> Than never to have loved at all.

If you've ever known someone who has given you nothing but pure love, whose whole being quivers with joy at the chance to be with you, who holds no grudges, harbors no anger or vindictiveness at your failings, has dedicated his entire life to adoring you, and then one day goes away forever, you know the depth of my grief.

You loved me well, my precious Kalu.

Now rest in peace.

Lessons of Dementia

There's a touching scene in the Ronald Harwood/Dustin Hoffman movie, *Quartet*, where Maggie Smith's character, Jean, a resident in a retirement home for gifted musicians, is faced with a dilemma. She and three other renowned opera singers are ready to go on stage for the finale of Giuseppe Verdi's birthday tribute, and sing the quartet from *Rigoletto*. Just then, fellow singer Cissy has an episode of sundown syndrome, the phenomenon where someone with dementia becomes suddenly disoriented, usually toward the end of the day. Cissy needs to find her luggage, she says, because it's time to leave.

The two gentlemen of the quartet alternate panic and frustration as they try to tell her she's wrong. She's not going anywhere, and she needs to hurry up and get on stage for their grand performance.

But Jean takes a different approach. "Yes, let's go get your bags," she says gently, as she takes Cissy's arm and leads her toward the door. She assures Cissy that she has plenty of time; the trip is still two weeks away.

With this small gesture, meeting her friend where she is, Jean has set Cissy's world right again.

Watching that scene brought back memories of a time this simple lesson—to meet people where they are—hit me squarely in the face.

My mother was well into her eighties when indications of a unique reality started to take over. Dementia affects people differently, some becoming more aggressive, others more docile. Most have strong memories of the days of yore yet few of the immediate past. In my mother's case, she became sweeter, mellower, more agreeable. She remembered a father who was proud of her, a music teacher who made her an accomplished cellist, and a husband who once said she was the best thing that ever happened to him.

But dementia's biggest gift to my mother, I believe, was that she began to live in the present. For her, the here and now was untainted by what causes stress for most people: fear of the future and regret over the past.

One year, I traveled from Denver, Colorado, to St. Paul, Minnesota, to be with my mother while her caretakers, my brother and his wife, took a vacation. On the first day, as the shadows of dusk began to darken the living room, Mom was tired of visiting.

"I need to go home now," she said. "Les won't know where I am."

"Oh, Mom," I protested. "Can't you stay? I came all the way from Colorado to see you." I knew not to mention that my dad had died ten years earlier.

"You did?" she said. A big smile spread across her face. "Well, if that's the case, of course I'll stay."

And we spent a pleasant evening, then turned in for the night.

On the second day, as the shadows of dusk once again began to darken the living room, Mom was tired of visiting.

"I need to go home now," she said. "Les won't know where I am."

"Oh, Mom," I said, hoping the same line would work. "Can't you stay? I came all the way from Colorado to see you."

"You did?" A big smile spread across her face. "Well, if that's the case, of course I'll stay."

And we spent a pleasant evening, then turned in for the night.

The next afternoon, just as dusk was flirting with the idea of darkening the living room, Mom became agitated.

"I need to go home," she demanded. "Right now."

"Can't you stay, Mom?" *One last time.* "I came all the way from Colorado to see you."

But this time, Mom didn't buy it. "Les is going to think something happened to me. I don't want to be here anymore. Take me home. Now. I've been here long enough." Her face tightened.

I had run out of distractions.

"Mom," was all I could say. "You *are* home. This is where you live now."

She looked at me like I had just announced she was a stick figure. She placed her hand on her tensed-up forehead and shook her head slowly.

"You people frustrate me. I can't make you understand me."

My heart melted with a compassion I had never tapped before.

What if, I wondered, *someone told me I wasn't really sitting there in my brother's living room, that I was instead in an igloo in Alaska? And worst of all, what if someone told me I didn't have a family waiting for me back in*

Colorado? What if the reality I knew was dismissed right and left, every time I spoke?

At that moment my heart grew three sizes, matching that of the Grinch at the moment of his transformation. And I now knew what to do.

"Okay, Mom," I said. "Let's get your hat and coat. I'm taking you home."

Ten minutes later, we were gliding on the packed ice of Minnesota streets on a February evening, Barnes & Noble the destination flashing on our GPS. As we slipped into the warmth of the bookstore, the aroma of Starbucks lattes seduced us.

"Would you like some coffee?" I offered.

She smiled serenely. "No, honey. I'll just sit over here." She sank into an easy chair and watched contentedly as several children flitted from bookshelf to bookshelf, energized by all their choices. I slipped a magazine onto her lap, and sat down in a chair next to hers.

We chatted, talking small about our lives, present and past.

"Where are you living now?" she asked.

"I'm in Denver, Mom."

"Oh, Denver. I hear that's a nice place. Les always said he would like to move to Denver."

She glanced down at her magazine, thumbed through a few pages, then looked up again.

"Where are you living now?" she asked me.

"I live in Denver."

"Oh, Denver. I hear that's a nice place. Les always said he would like to move to Denver. I wonder why we never did."

"It's a *really* great place, Mom. I can't imagine living anywhere else."

"Oh, that's nice." She looked around at our fellow booklovers, now removing their coats to settle in.

"Where are you living now, Margaret?"

"I live in Denver."

"Oh, I have a daughter in Denver."

Thirty minutes later, her interest in the setting was waning.

"Come on, Mom. Let's go back home," I said.

She looked pleased. "That's a good idea."

The brief ride home was comfortable and quiet. We turned at the familiar alley and pulled into my brother's garage.

"Careful. It's slippery," I said as I tucked my mother's arm through my own and led her into the house. We brushed the snow off our coats.

"We're home now, Mom," I announced, feeling smug that I had executed such a ruse, and outwitted sundown syndrome.

But Mom was one up on me.

She handed me her coat to hang up and sat down to slip off her boots. Then, with a tinge of boasting in her voice, she zinged me with a slightly arrogant huff: "Well. It took some doing, but at least I got what I wanted."

In her reality, in the here and now, my mom was home. In that moment, all was right with her world.

How healing is this simple concept, meeting people where they are? Not only those with dementia, but everyone.

It's just another name for respect.

The years I spent counseling, the decades I taught in schools and workplaces, and my lifetime of raising children, all provided me daily reminders of this truth. We're each on a journey, each in a different place—not better or worse, just different—and learning as we go. As my friend Tom always said in his slow, gentle cadence, "We're all just trying to get through life as best we can."

I've come to realize the most compassionate support I can give other people is to acknowledge that they are, at any given moment, exactly where they should be.

And if you're feeling unsteady, take my arm. We'll start where you are and move forward.

Vanished Memories

My computer crashed last week.

Sadly, the Mac Geniuses were not able to retrieve my lost data.

Such crises evoke unpredictable reactions. The first one was to cry. Then I kicked myself. Then I went to bed.

It was six thirty.

The nightmare that awaited me tried to hold me hostage in condemnation for not backing up my data. Mercifully, I stayed wide awake, in full control of my thoughts, taking inventory of all I'd lost. That was torment enough. Ominous images of my now-missing desktop icons swirled madly, darkly in my mind. Tax records, the schedule for an upcoming family reunion, an estimate for a bay window. Blog entries I'd been working to polish up. Valuable notes from an important class. A list of folks who could finish a basement. Client invoices, my hospice volunteer report template, a bunch of quotes by comparative mythologist Joseph Campbell that had recently taken on new meaning for me. All the bits and bytes of my life, gone. But it wasn't the end of the world. It was just data, after all, and I could get some of it back.

But I cringed at the more personal stuff.

Like the stories my dyslexic students had dictated to me: creative chronicles of their childhood imaginations, complete with illustrations. Gone. Crumpled up and swallowed by a destabilized data disk drive.

The letters my great-grandmother—outspoken Granny, who had a yen for chewing tobacco—had written in the 1800s, scanned and ready to weave into my memoirs. Years of rich history gobbled up in a momentary hiccup of that modern convenience called a computer.

And the photos I lost? More history, but of the kind I witnessed.

I was there, donned in my orange volunteer tee shirt at the 2008 Democratic National Convention in Denver, Colorado, witnessing the nomination of our country's first African-American president. I got him front and center at the podium at Mile High Stadium saying, "Yes, we can." Wiped away were the pixels to remember this by.

I was there with my family in 2009 in Iowa, only the third state to recognize equality for all. You know, forward-thinking Iowa. Ushered into the state by wind turbines, we witnessed my niece's wedding to her fiancée. The images I captured of two radiant young women making history, elegant in their ivory wedding dresses and so sincere in their dedication to each other, were now smoldering in my fried hard drive.

The complete loss of these vestiges of my life haunts me. I had pictures of people I care about deeply, from my past and my present, all whom I hope to see again, but some whom I almost certainly won't.

I had recorded my five summers holed up at Jersey Jim, during my two-day adventures playing fire ranger in the decommissioned lookout tower in southwest Colorado.

I had snapped shot after shot of the one item on my bucket list I thought I would never get to do, mainly because, incredulously, every one of the two dozen people I invited had politely—but with a surreptitious roll of the eyes—declined. Finally, I asked my sister Mary, who said, "Of course, I'd love to go zip lining! Why didn't you ask before?" On Maui, no less.

And the trip I call my "Eat, Pray, Love" journey: when a friend cancelled a road trip we had planned together, I was forced to drive up the California coast on my own, snapping plenty of photos along the way so that others could share in my wonderment.

And the other trips. All the beauty and excitement of Vancouver, Banff, Montreal, Quebec City, Yosemite, southern California, Washington, D.C., Philadelphia and nearby Amish country, Seattle, the Twin Cities, New Orleans, Santa Fe, Moab, my childhood home in Idaho, all the highlights of my own state of Colorado.

I'll spend the next several years putting my digital life back together. But in the meantime, I've accepted the technological advice of those who want to save me the exasperation of ever going through this again: Back. Up. Your. Stuff.

I probably should have followed the advice my son Andrew gave me years ago: "Mom, why don't you put down the camera and just savor it all?" And since the incident, that's exactly what I've done. In remembrance of files lost, I've made it a point to savor every moment.

At the conclusion of Marisa Silver's superb novel *Mary Coin*, Walker, the descendant of a depression-era single mother trying to survive in the fields of California, whose photographed image would burn in the psyches of generations to come, brought me solace.

"There is always a yearning in the piecing together of information," Walker reflected. "Something happened here once. Something that might have gone unnoticed but for a person with a camera."

Yet "it's a photograph, an alchemy of fact and invention that produces something recognizable as the truth. But it is not the truth."

As he watched the photo enter the trash icon of his laptop, Walker closed with his final insight. "It will always exist. In a cloud. In an invisible language of zeroes and ones. There is no erasure."

And so it is.

Second Glass
BUBBLY

Bubbly

I was lying in bed, tucked into that brief pocket of time between wakeup and getup, shards of morning color splashed across the bedspread. My newborn daughter lay on my stomach, sleeping soundly. Keeping my previous four children out of the parental bed during infancy had deprived me of sleep and sanity for years, and I'd finally realized that bringing my youngest into bed with me after her way-too-early morning feeding would afford me, if not extra sleep, at least a little reflection time before the rest of the household awoke.

Thoughts, memories, and insights didn't waste any time bubbling up, tumbling around like stained-glass beads in a kaleidoscope. One in particular found my funny bone, tickling me as surely as fingers on my ribs. It filled me with silent glee.

All of a sudden, that little baby sat up and let out a deep, hearty belly laugh that filled the room like music in a cathedral. Then just as suddenly, she rested her head back on my tummy and resumed her slumber.

With that extraordinary connection, my merriment multiplied.

Studies are telling us that those giggles are a vital part of a baby's cognitive development. They are a marker of social and emotional engagement, and an important form of communication. "Laughter," said Danish comedian and musician Victor Borge, "is the shortest distance between two people."

But those in their later years are also influenced by the power of lightheartedness. When my friend Mike was diagnosed with cancer, I racked my brain for something I could do for him. And then it came: a series of "Laugh with Mike" parties. He and his wife understood exactly why I suggested it, as did Mike's friends. Nothing about our parties was irreverent; on the contrary, our intention was to release Mike's healing endorphins and hurl that cancer out of his soma-sphere. My research had shown that laughter strengthens the immune system, boosts energy, diminishes pain, and protects one from the damaging effects of stress. We could only trust that those hidden benefits were at play in Mike after our parties, but what was obvious was that our cheery gatherings created intimacy, happiness, and hopefulness for our friend. He knew we were rooting for him.

Opportunities to take the serious lightly abound. Even if a situation doesn't evoke outright roaring laughter, simply adopting a more playful, more jovial, more tongue-in-cheek take on the obstacles and setbacks we encounter in life can achieve the same effect.

The vignettes that follow strive to do just that. To be sure, if lightheartedness heals, energizes, and bonds, then let our lives be bubbly.

The Legend of James and James in St. James

Rich family folklore can instill pride in a person, regardless of whether the events they recount actually happened. Among my kin, pride came from the enduring presence of cowboys throughout the generations.

I always knew my dad had once been a cowboy. Not only did he make us cowboy potatoes for dinner, but on top of my parents' dresser was a framed, black-and-white photo of Dad sitting atop a horse and wearing a ten-gallon hat. No matter that he was in the process of studying the ecology of Rocky Mountain bighorn sheep in Utah for his doctoral dissertation—as far as I was concerned, he was Hopalong Cassidy.

But before Dad's stint in the Wild West, and perhaps the inspiration for it, oral tradition in the family had created a legend around my great-grandfather, James McCann, who one day had encountered the American outlaw, gang leader, bank and train robber, and murderer Jesse James.

History doesn't dispute the basics. Missouri-born Jesse James and his brother Frank were Confederate guerrillas during the Civil War, loathed and feared for atrocities they committed against Union soldiers. When the real combat was over, they continued their own personal war by forming a gang that took part in robberies of anything and everything—banks, stagecoaches, trains, planes, automobiles, and maybe even defenseless mom-and-pop store owners—until 1876, when their attempted robbery of a bank in Northfield, Minnesota, resulted in the capture or deaths of several gang members. We know that Jesse James and his dastardly desperados continued their crime spree after Northfield, actively recruiting new members even with The Law hot on their trail. But on April 3, 1882, it all came to an end when gang member Robert Ford murdered Jesse James in hopes of collecting a reward.

Those are the facts.

This is also true: It was on their way to Northfield that Jesse James and his gang stopped for groceries at my great-grandfather James

McCann's market near St. James, Minnesota, in 1876. Okay, the fact that there are so many Jameses in the story might seem suspicious, but it's the gospel truth.

Now, that's all we know for sure.

However, a generation later, my Grandpa Edward and his sons, one of whom was my dad, entertained themselves by surmising what they thought might—nay, must—have been the story behind the story. So they spent many an evening postulating.

Grandpa Edward speculated that his father, James, the storekeeper who had provided groceries to Jesse James, had overheard James and his thugs discussing their upcoming Northfield heist while manhandling the tomatoes they were about to buy for their sandwiches. His eyes cast downward, Great-Grandpa James sidled over to the corn bin where he would not be seen and, pretending to sort the fresh-picked ears into a golden display, overheard the whole plan. Then, right after the gang had ridden out of town and the last of the dust had settled, James McCann notified the authorities.

How else would the sheriff and his posse have been at the Northfield bank at exactly the time of the attempted robbery?

But the intrigue deepens.

Shortly after the Northfield raid, James McCann moved his wife and children to a new location, while he himself stayed in St. James.

Why?

Why, indeed.

The only possible explanation: James McCann knew that Jesse James had gotten to wondering how The Law in Northfield was able to figure out they were coming. Enraged that his partners had faced such brutality, and having narrowly escaped death himself, Jesse James was out for revenge.

The outlaw's mind turned to the only possible person who could have known about their plans: that good-for-nothing snitch at the food market in St. James. He'd hunt him down, the varmint, and show him that you do not mess with Jesse James.

So Great-Grandpa James, intuiting Jesse James's intentions, shuttled his wife and young'uns north to a nameless location near

Minneapolis for their safety. Then, his horse rearing, he galloped south again to bravely face the possibility that he himself might one day be shot down by that lowlife Jesse James.

That's the legend that has been passed down through the generations. History may dispute it, but in my mind, those are the facts.

And yes, I do feel a blush of pride.

Identity Crisis

What might be most striking about me is the number of names I've used over the years. My mother, tapping her inner poet, liked sonorous names that also had rhythm.

She christened my older sister Catherine McCann, the /k/ and /n/ sounds in both names clearly alluring. When I was born, she debated between Barbara and Margaret. While Barbara flowed better, Margaret brought alliteration into the mix. So Margaret McCann I became, purely for the timbre. Subsequent McCann girls received melodious monikers as well: Mary Maureen McCann and Therese Anne McCann.

The boys, on the other hand, were dubbed for distinction. Brother Number One barely escaped Reginald, at Dad's insistence. They eventually agreed upon George, which sufficiently rang of royalty. Doug was next, named for General Douglas MacArthur, a hero to my patriotic father.

The baby, Charlie, was supposed to be Carl Morgan McCann, my mother's effort to memorialize her dad. Things took a turn for the better, however, because of me. I was seventeen years old at the time, and I had a colossal crush on a boy named Chuck. "How about Charles?" I suggested. "Carl is kind of old-fashioned." Mom eventually granted my wish, which had to be a huge concession on her part. Either that or it, too, rang of royalty.

So there we were: Catherine, Margaret, George, Douglas, Mary, Therese, and Charles. Great names one and all.

The problem was that second child.

I was seven years old when I realized I didn't like my name. I hated saying it and hated hearing it. I was not, at my core, a Margaret.

Yes, in a giant cosmic blunder, I had been misnamed.

This may all seem laughable, but for me, my name was truly a burden.

Right around that time, my sister Cathy, inspired by *Little Women*, started calling me Meg, and George followed suit. But to the rest of the family, nuclear and extended, I was still Margaret. And being a parochial school student didn't help: most Catholic children had saints' names, and, as befitted saints, we were all called by our formal names.

In seventh grade, however, I got a reprieve. My teacher took the liberty of addressing me as Peggy, and my classmates joined right in. So for a year, I was Peggy McCann. An enormous relief.

At the end of that school year in St. Paul, Minnesota, however, our family moved across town. I left my friends—and my nickname—at St. Luke's Grade School and became an eighth-grader at Nativity Grade School.

Within a week, the girls pulled me aside and said, "No offense, but Margaret is not a very cool name. We need to do something about that." They decided I would be Mickie, short for McCann. I now bore a suitable name for middle school, and Mickie McCann I remained even through high school and college.

Fast forward.

On a cool and exceptionally brilliant Midwest day in September, firm in my identity as Mickie McCann, I strode into my college classroom. Mystically, my eyes were drawn like magnets to an irresistible young man with a typical 1960s look: moustache, sideburns, and bell-bottom jeans. I sidled over to the empty chair next to him and plopped down, amazed at my boldness.

"Hi, I'm Mickie," I declared with feigned confidence.

"Hi, Maggie. I'm Steve," my new crush countered.

Maggie. He called me Maggie.

My mind raced in circles like mice in a maze. *What do I do?* Too timid to tell him he had heard me wrong, I kept quiet.

And that's how I became Maggie.

Steve and I eventually married, so Maggie was there to stay. I couldn't get my parents and siblings to jump on the Maggie bandwagon, and I could hardly convince my decades' worth of friends to get *off* the Maggie bandwagon, so I remained a woman of many names.

To this day, though "Maggie" leads the pack, I still answer to Meg, Margaret, Mickie, Mom, Miss Maggie, Ms. Pike, Magness, Maggers, and, as I trained my elementary students to call me, Mrs. Pike, Master of Arts, Your Highness.

At times, it's hard to keep it all straight. But the best part about all this, in light of my married name, is that Peggy didn't stick. Peggy Pike . . . what, picked a peck of pickled peppers?

    Please.

Vigilante

It was 1968 when I took the law into my own hands.

I had a part-time job as a cashier at Hove's Supermarket in the Highland area of St. Paul, Minnesota, an upper-crust neighborhood near my family's own modest middle-class home. I had worked at Hove's since I was sixteen, my first and only job before my professional career started. Of all my girlfriends who worked elsewhere, I was the highest paid, thanks to required membership in the Amalgamated Meat Cutters Union. Even though I never sliced a single shank during my tenure at Hove's, I was glad to join those who did. Those Hove's checks paid for my college tuition, as well as for many years of clothes and entertainment.

The Sunday before I became a vigilante, I settled into the green velvet wingback chair in my family's spacious, gold-walled living room to read the *St. Paul Pioneer Press*. The *Parade* insert held a tantalizing headline on the cover, and I quickly paged through until I located the article. There it was: "Quick-Change Artists: How They Work."

I thought I had heard that expression before, quick-change artist. Images sprang to mind of Snidely Whiplash swiftly changing costumes—from dark-caped villain, twisting his moustache, to elderly gentleman hobbling on a cane— as a ruse to trick the innocent Nell Fenwick.

But as I read on, I learned something new. A quick-change artist was someone who tried to swindle store clerks out of money by quickly and repeatedly asking for change before the cashier could think about it, ultimately absconding with more than he or she came in with.

For example, the quick-changer would purchase a $1 box of tea (a respectable purchase in those days), and hand the clerk $20. Now read this part quickly to get the full effect of how fast a quick-change artist works: The clerk gives the con artist $19 in change. He then gives her back the $10 bill and asks for two twenties, which she gives him. Then he takes the $5 bill and another $20 bill and asks for three tens. She complies, whereupon he gives it right back and asks for eight fives because he owes his mother and daughter money and also has to buy gas and needs the exact amount. She understands his predicament, and hands over the fives.

The quick-change artist thanks the cashier and calmly leaves, tucking the $65 he just collected into his back pocket. The clerk suspects nothing until her boss informs her the next day that her till was short. She still doesn't know how it happened.

The story made such an impact on me that it was still twirling in my mind the following Saturday when I donned my pink Hove's uniform and showed up for my daylong shift at the register. In the late afternoon, after a draining day on my feet, with numbers and cash register buttons swimming before my eyes, I greeted my next customer. He only had one item, which was a welcome sight after hours and hours of ringing up one massive pile of groceries after another.

"Hello!" I said in my cheeriest voice.

My bleary eyes identified the one item he had: a small box of tea.

An alarm went off inside me. I was immediately suspicious. His appearance was the first giveaway. A scrawny man, unshaven and scruffy, he was wearing tattered jeans and a blue, plaid shirt that had probably never seen an iron.

Gourmet tea? Really?

I couldn't be sure this guy was going to try to rip me off, but I was ready. I quickly reviewed all the information I had learned in the article about quick-change artists.

Bring it on.

"How are you, little lady?" he said.

Don't talk to me like that.

"Fine," I replied curtly, but just politely enough to meet the minimum customer service guidelines.

"Will that be all?" I half-mumbled, flinging his tin of Constant Comment into a bag.

Of course that will be all. He's a quick-change artist. He's here for money, not tea.

In the background, muffled by my sleuthy thoughts, the customer was babbling on and on about who-even-knew-what.

Uh-huh. Distracting me, is he?

"Ahem," I interrupted. "That'll be three dollars."

"An exact amount!" he exclaimed. "I bet that doesn't happen very often."

Gads, it happens all the time. Do you know how many people say that?

He dug into his wallet.

Watch, the scoundrel will hand me a twenty.

He handed me a twenty.

I smiled condescendingly. "Four, five, and five is ten, and ten is twenty," I recited as I forked the bills over into his waiting hand. "You have a great day."

He turned to walk away. I braced myself.

"On second thought . . ." he said, turning back around.

I knew it! He couldn't be waltzing more predictably into my script if he tried.

"Give me two fives for this ten. I owe my wife some money, and . . ."—I mentally mouthed the end of the sentence with him—*I need exact change*. I took his ten and gave him two fives. He turned to leave.

"Oh!" the rogue blurted out, spinning around to face me yet again. He pulled out another bill. "Could I get—"

"No," I said. *He's going to give me a ten and ask for two twenties. Does he think I'm stupid?*

"What?"

"I said no."

"Wh-why?" He looked confused. *Right.*

"Because I know what you're doing," I said. *Good God. Where did I get this nerve? I can't believe I'm saying this.*

The crook winced. "What do you mean? What am I doing?"

I stared him down for a few very long seconds.

"You know what you're doing," I said, pausing for dramatic effect. "And so do I."

The good-for-nothing put his bill away. "No, I would never do that. That's not what I'm doing. Don't say I'm doing that."

He looked hurt, but I knew it was an act. *The swindler doth protest too much, methinks.*

And with that, he slunk out the front door of Hove's Highland Grocery, never to be seen again. We got him, *Parade* and I.

Abysmal Anosmia

Every time I play "Three Truths and a Lie," I say the same thing:

> 1. I used to be able to fly anywhere in the world for almost nothing.
> 2. I once belonged to the Amalgamated Meat Cutters Union.
> 3. I'm a gourmet chef.
> 4. I can't smell.

The truth:

> 1. True. My son used to be a pilot. The airlines were good to moms.
> 2. True. For six years, high school through college. But I wasn't a butcher; I sliced bread and sold cakes right next to the meat counter.
> 3. Oh, please. People who know me just laugh that I would even try to pull this one off.
> 4. True. I can't smell, I never could smell, and it's unlikely I'll ever be able to smell.

There's even a word for my condition—I googled it.
I have anosmia.

I was a child of eight when I realized something was amiss. My sister was having a birthday party, and my mother planned a "sniff test" as an activity. A dozen substances in jars sat on the table, and we had to identify each one by scent. My nose hovered above the first item. I breathed in, as I saw the others doing. Nothing. I moved on to the next. Nothing. And the next. Still nothing.

What am I doing wrong? What does smelling feel like? All the other girls were sniffing away and jotting down words, so I did the only thing I *could* do: I faked it.

Since I was in my own house, I had an advantage. While all the guests were busy smelling, I was busy picturing the several items my mother had set out on the kitchen counter before the party. *Vanilla, coffee, Karo syrup, and . . . oh! Mustard.* When the tests were graded, I, the only anosmic in the group, was the winner, having scored 100 percent on the sniff test.

I've studied up on my condition. Researchers from the University of Dresden Medical School in Germany found that participants born without a sense of smell experienced more insecurity in social situations and were at increased risk of depression than those in control groups.

Well, duh. You would be, too, if you had to explain—constantly—why you can't get ecstatic over the perfume someone's holding up to your nose. Or to answer, repeatedly, the inevitable question, "So, does that mean you can't taste either?" Really now, do I look like someone who can't taste? Or to listen longingly as everyone raves about the delightful smell of rain. To be on the outside when people wax nostalgic about the glorious childhood memories certain smells evoke. To stand there awkwardly when someone asks, "What's that smell? Pee-yew!"—praying they're not talking about your breath or armpits.

It's abysmal being anosmic.

Of course, there are advantages to not being able to smell. When I taught in a sixth grade classroom of twenty-five youngsters who had not yet discovered deodorant, and a visitor walked in one day only to do an immediate about-face before tearing out of the room with her nose covered, I could go right on teaching, wondering why the histrionics. On road trips when my family would suddenly scream "Ewwwww!"—apparently skunks don't smell very good—I could continue admiring the scenery uninterrupted. And the rank odor of livestock permeating Greeley, Colorado? Doesn't bother me at all.

But anosmia can also have dire consequences. Like the time in seventh grade when I was babysitting, and the woman from the apartment upstairs came down to tell me she smelled gas—it seemed the kids had been playing with the knobs on the gas stove.

Or the time I was studying at my kitchen table, and looked up to see the whole room full of smoke from the oven—I'd been so absorbed in my homework, I didn't even notice. And the next day when I had to clean said oven, I inhaled the noxious fumes as if they were fresh oxygen, only to suffer a horrendous headache that lasted four days.

So this is the truth I have to live with, and sometimes, frankly, it stinks.

Or at least I think it does.

Gawky Prom Date

It was April of junior year, and at Our Lady of Peace High School in St. Paul, Minnesota, the day of our Junior-Senior Prom was looming.

With the exception of our friend Lauren, not one of my circle of friends had a real boyfriend. The rest of us—let's just say it—had to scrounge for boys to take to "J-S."

But one by one, some of the girls found dates, and two weeks before the dance, only three of us remained wallflowers.

That's when my dad stepped in. "You do know no boy is going to pick up the phone and invite himself, don't you?"

"But I don't have anyone to ask," I whined. "I guess Rita, Jan, and I will just go to a movie that night."

"I could ask Father McGrath if he'd find a boy from St. Thomas College to go with you. He's in charge of the dormitories."

"Don't you dare!" I screamed. *Egad, could it get any more embarrassing than this?*

The next day my friends and I were sitting in the Tea Room—which is what my high school, with a straight face, called its cafeteria—and I grumbled that I had reached rock bottom: my *father* had offered to fix me up for J-S.

"Really?" said Jan, her eyes lighting up.

"Do you think he could find two guys?" added Rita.

"Or three?" Jan piped in.

I sank my teeth into my apple. *They're talking crazy.*

"I already have a date," said Debbie. "But if I didn't, I would kill to take a college guy to J-S."

"Do it," urged Lauren. "I've gone out with college men." *Of course.*

I wrapped my apple core back in its waxed paper and stuffed it into my bag.

"You think?" I finally said. "You mean you really want my dad to find dates for us?"

They did.

So Dad came home one day with news that three college

freshmen—Tim, Mark, and Beau—had visited him in his office at the college to volunteer for the job. After making sure one of them was sufficiently tall for me, Dad and I matched Jan with Beau, Rita with Mark, and me with Tim. Now we were ready to join our friends in the whirl of prom preparation.

Tradition at OLP was to gather at someone's house for a "Coketail party" for pictures and introductions. Rita, Jan, and I would meet our dates for the first time right beforehand.

Oh. My. Gosh.

What we saw when we opened the door set our stomachs grinding and our hearts aflutter.

These were three of the most gorgeous men we'd ever seen. And the tuxes didn't hurt. Tim was tall, dark, and handsome; Mark was blond, cute, and sweet; Beau was an attractive, mirthful teddy bear.

Problem was, we didn't know how to act in the presence of such splendor. How do you talk to an Adonis?

When we walked into the Coketail party, Mary, Patti, Trudy, Joelle, Debbie, and Lauren each took turns gliding over to let us know how lucky we were.

Lucky? That's not how the three of us felt. More like tongue-tied. Self-conscious. Gawky. It was going to be a long evening.

The dance itself was in the Radisson Hotel ballroom. Sister Mary Celestine had issued ample warning that the nuns would have handkerchiefs with them to stuff into any plunging necklines, so we glided into the sea of girls attired in high-necked, empire waist dresses, arms covered by long, elegant Jackie Kennedy gloves.

The yearbook later gave full-page coverage to Jan and Beau, and Rita and Mark sitting romantically at the edge of the fountain outside the ballroom. No one had to know the story behind the picture: that neither girl had spoken barely a word the whole evening. Meanwhile, Tim and I were on the dance floor, I stepping on his feet, he no doubt wondering what to talk about with such a horrendously shy girl.

A story such as this, The Girls' First Prom, should reach a dramatic climax, either with someone falling in love or with a comical—or even horrifying—gaffe. *Something.*

But no.

The story befits the three of us perfectly: It simply falls flat. Tim, Mark, and Beau took us home and faded into college life, never to be seen again.

Way out of our league, those guys.

But that's what you get when you stoop to letting your dad scrounge for your dates.

Teenage Drama

As a sixteen-year-old girl who normally shunned theatrics, I suddenly found myself craving it. Life had become a bit monotonous, and all I needed was something—*anything*—to foster a little angst during my teenage years. To create longing. To grip me.

So I needed drama. But I also needed pathos. And maybe some aching passion.

I found it all in the movie *Shenandoah*.

Set during the Civil War, it told the story of Charlie Anderson, played by Jimmy Stewart, who held firm to his anti-war stance with his repeated refusals to send his sons into a conflict that "doesn't concern us"—that is, until his youngest son, Boy, was captured by Union soldiers.

Shenandoah came out at exactly the right time in my life, just when I had started yearning for some emotional intensity. I was in Corpus Christi, Texas, on a trip with my family to visit relatives. My cousin and a couple of his friends took my siblings and me to the movies one night. It may be because Raymond and his buddies were so much older, but I felt like I needed to allow—no, *force*—this movie to tap something deep inside me. *Shenandoah* touched on the morality of war, the tension between patriotism and humanitarianism, familial bonds, human rights, and the role of faith in crisis—all concepts we'd talked about in my high school classes and Film Study Club.

In other words, drama. Pathos. Aching passion.

Two hours in, by the time Boy Anderson, supported by a ragged crutch, hobbled down the church aisle to the strains of "Praise Father, Son, and Holy Ghost," I was a dam broken. After the movie, the others, apparently unmoved but anxious to dry my tears, joked and wisecracked the raw fervor right out of me.

But I still had my friends at school.

"Oh my gosh, you guys," I gasped the minute we'd gathered in the Tea Room for lunch. "I saw the best movie. We have to go. Like, Saturday night we have to go."

My zeal, of course, gave my friends no choice.

"Okay, where are we going?" one of them asked.

I'd done my research. "Minneapolis. That's the only place it's playing."

Venturing across the Mississippi River and into downtown Minneapolis was like going to Broadway in New York—it was a big deal. As in, wear a dress and maybe even have dinner at Jax Café beforehand big deal.

At the theater, we all settled into our seats. I, knowing what was going to happen, began to cry from the very first scene. Luscious, soaking tears poured out of me like a sponge being squeezed dry. By the time we exited the theater, I was sufficiently anguished, as the teenager I wanted to be should have been.

But looking around, I saw too many dry eyes. What I desperately wanted was a fellow drama queen who would share my love of *Shenandoah*. Someone equally gripped by the plight of Jimmy Stewart and his southern clan.

Joelle stepped up to the plate.

Joelle loved *Shenandoah*. She and I would see the movie another ten times before we graduated and left St. Paul. But that night, we immediately hopped into Joelle's Volkswagen Bug and drove straight to Schmidt's Music to buy the record.

"Okay, we'll trade every week. You can keep it first." Joelle handed me the treasured 78-rpm vinyl disc and watched with envy as I fingered the stark, yellow-orange-and-black cover. The characters had become our friends, and Joelle and I felt no shame at the tears we shed seeing Ann and James in their last embrace; Jenny whispering goodbye to her love, Sam; and Charlie Anderson, jaw firm, gripping his rifle as he growled his seminal change of heart in deliberate cadence: "*Now* it concerns us." Every once in a while, Joelle and I would clear our throats, lower our voices, and punch out Jimmy Stewart's words: "If we don't *try*, we don't *do*. And if we don't *do*, then why are we here on this earth?" Stewart at his finest. Does it get any more grip-worthy than that?

Regrettably, the album disappeared over the years. After playing it a good one or two hundred times between the two of us on our cheap record players, it developed a few scratches. Then sadly, like Puff the Magic Dragon, our *Shenandoah* record slipped into some phantom cave far away from the corners of the country where Joelle and I drifted.

Little did we know that a decade later, we would both be living in Southern California, Joelle married to the U.S. Marines, I married to many years of graduate school.

One day, Joelle called. "Hey, let's celebrate our birthdays this year," she suggested. Joelle and I were born two days apart. "Can you believe we're already three decades old?"

"Ouch, Joelle. Shut up," I said. "But come on over. We'll figure out something to do."

Joelle arrived early that afternoon with her sons, Joseph and Andy, in tow. My own Timothy and Anne were waiting, ready to escort their playmates to the toy room. Joelle went back out to her car and returned carrying a big box wrapped in ribbons and glitter that wouldn't stop.

"This is for us," Joelle said.

"Hmm." I carefully untied the ribbons on the rectangular shirt box. *Something for us. Matching tee shirts maybe? Paperbacks to pass back and forth?*

"Oh, just hurry up," said Joelle as she ripped the paper off herself and lifted the lid.

I blinked in disbelief.

The flat, cardboard record cover flashed its bright, yellow-orange-and-black label, nearly blinding me.

I shrieked. "Where did you find this, Joelle?"

"My mother sent it to me when she sold the house. It was in the back of my closet, I guess."

Within minutes Joelle and I were settled in easy chairs, the din of our children in the background, the melody of "Shenandoah" filling the living room.

Drama. Pathos. Aching passion. It was nothing short of solemn.

"Ahem," said Joelle, lowering her voice a few octaves. "If we don't *try*, we don't *do* . . ."

I joined her. "And if we don't *do*, then why are we here on this earth?"

We hadn't lost it. Still gripped, that's what we were, Joelle and I.

Hotel Problematic

When four of us decided to take a road trip to Jackson Hole, Wyoming, for its annual writers' conference, we expected only good to come out of it. Before we get too far, I want you to know that I didn't do anything to provoke the desk clerk at the hotel. I really didn't. I had nothing but goodwill in my heart.

How could I not? As we approached the Grand Tetons, looming over the horizon in all their majesty, I was struck with a serenity so sudden it made me gasp. "Bob, you have to stop this car right now," I said. "Sorry, everyone. I can hardly breathe, it's so stunning. I have to take this in."

Bob stopped the car and I went into a trance, staring at those peaks where the sun danced just right to reflect off the glaring, white snow.

This was definitely foreshadowing. I knew if our Creator could fashion this utter splendor, then it would be nothing for her to orchestrate our signing on with agents this weekend, publishing best sellers, and generating so much income that we could spend our remaining days visiting spectacular places like Teton National Park.

And if not that, then at least an agreeable stay at a comfortable Wyoming hotel.

We headed south into Jackson, a tiny western town right out of Marshal Matt Dillon's *Gunsmoke*. A stroll along the wooden walkways gave us the lay of the land: bars, shops, inns, restaurants, and lots of cowboy hats. In the middle of town, an arc of elk horns adorned the entrance to George Washington Memorial Park. After touring this charming venue, which was sure to cause a deluge of creative writing juices, we thought we'd better get settled in at our hotel. Thanks to the internet, we had already secured rooms right around the corner from the modern event center in Jackson, where the conference would take place.

We approached the hotel with, as I said, nothing but goodwill in our hearts. Stacy greeted us at the front desk. Sweet, blond, cute, perky, and young, Stacy gave us our keys and sent us on our way.

My friend and I walked into our room—and saw chaos. The beds were unmade, trash cans full, towels strewn about, takeout cups and containers everywhere.

"Oops, is this the wrong room?" my friend asked.

"I don't know. Let's go ask Stacy."

Stacy was bewildered. The cleaners had apparently missed our room.

"I'll have this clean in no time," she promised. "Have you had dinner yet? Maybe you could do that. Oh, and there's a reenactment of a shootout down the street you might like. When you get back, your room will be ready."

"No problem," I assured her.

But before we could walk out the front door, a young man, the other hotel clerk, approached us.

"Hi, I'm Josh. Listen, Stacy and I were talking, and we'd like to make this inconvenience up to you. We have our luxury suite upstairs that I know you'll like. Follow me."

We grabbed our suitcases and followed Josh... *outside*? Apparently, the only way up was a winding, wrought iron staircase, which was all of twelve inches wide. Josh nimbly ascended, but—and here was the only problem—the two of us had to figure out how to squeeze ourselves and our bags between the railings of the narrow walkway. So we lifted our suitcases over our heads, turned sideways, and walked like crabs up the fifteen steps to the balcony.

No problem.

When we caught up to Josh, he was jiggling the keys in the lock, trying to open the door.

"I know they work. It's just that sometimes . . . " He grunted.

No problem. A minute or two went by. *Right?*

Suddenly, Josh swung the door open, beaming with pleasure at the suite he was offering us. The one he knew we would love.

"Well, you two enjoy this suite. It's about twice the price of your room downstairs, but we won't charge you. It was our mistake."

"No problem, Josh," I said. "Thank you."

But there was just one problem: the room was suffocating. I shuffled across the sterile, industrial carpet, into the bedroom, and headed straight for the air conditioner, only to find that the knobs were covered over with duct tape.

"Oh gee. Look at this." My roommate and I started snickering at the thought of this being the "luxury" suite.

"Look, I'll take the couch in the living room, and you can have the bedroom," I said. "I'll just keep the windows open and see if we can cool this place down."

The sun set shortly after we settled in, and the wide windows provided a fine breeze. The only problem was that they opened right onto the balcony, which was fully accessible to the general public via the winding staircase. It was unnerving to think that anyone could climb up those stairs, walk onto the balcony, and step over the six-inch window base, right into the living room where I would be sleeping. Also, the windows faced the main drag, the one with all the bars and cowboy hats. But no problem. I had nothing but goodwill in my heart, remember. I tried to doze off.

The only other problem was that the busy main street in Jackson, Wyoming, was bustling with activity—as in all night long. Motorcycles flooring, beverages pouring, cowboys roaring. I lay on the hide-a-bed wide awake, metal bar digging into my back, waiting for the sun to rise and release me from this misery. *No problem,* I thought. *I can do this for one night.*

In the morning I was awakened by a loud shriek from the bathroom. "I can't believe this! Maggie, come look at this!"

My lower back groaned as I extricated myself from the metal frame of the bed—covered by what could hardly be called a mattress—that I had slept on all night. One hand on my back, I hobbled into the bathroom, where my suitemate was running the shower, waiting for it to heat up.

"Look."

Inside the shower stall was the toilet paper roll. Not *a* toilet paper roll. *The* toilet paper roll.

And not *next* to the shower, *inside* the shower. Meaning *right under* the stream of water. And it wasn't just that someone had absent-mindedly thrown the roll in there, or accidentally left it on the edge of the tub. No, whoever had built the shower had actually constructed an indented shelf, fully tiled, expressly for the purpose of holding a roll of toilet paper.

No problem. We'll just get another roll from the cabinet and let this one dry out.

So let's review: Tight, winding staircase, nonfunctioning air conditioner, outside entrance directly into the living room, cacophony all night long, and now toilet paper holder in the shower. I sure hoped our original room would be ready for the second night.

The only problem was we couldn't find Stacy before we left for the conference in the morning. Surely, though, she would let us know as soon as we could move out of the luxury suite, with a note on the door, perhaps, or a phone call to the room. Oh, wait a minute—there *was* no phone in the room.

So the second night was much like the first.

This was bordering on problematic.

On the second day of the conference, we had a midmorning break, giving me a chance to check my cell phone for messages.

"Ms. Pike. This is Stacy from your hotel. You never checked with me about moving back into the room you actually reserved. We gave you the luxury suite as an apology for not having your room ready, but I distinctly told you—three times—to get back to me about moving into the smaller room. My phone's ringing off the hook with people who want to rent the luxury suite, and I've had to turn them down because *you didn't get back to me.*"

Then her voice took on a "neener-neener" tone.

"But that's okay because I have your credit card number. I've charged you for last night and I'll charge you for every night you stay there. So since you didn't tell me you wanted to go back to the smaller room, I guess that means you don't mind paying twice as much for the luxury suite. If you don't want to be charged for another night, you'd better get your things out of that suite by eleven o'clock."

It was ten thirty already, so I left the conference, quickly walked back to the hotel, squeezed myself onto that winding staircase again, and made four trips up and down those blasted steps to bring all of our bags down.

This was a problem.

To gauge how Stacy was doing, I brought up a mental list of the good customer service strategies I had learned at my first part-time job:

1. Be pleasant. *No.*
2. Clear up misunderstandings. *Huh-uh.*
3. Help in any way you can. (Stacy did offer to carry some bags—once I had brought them all downstairs. *Thanks a lot.*)
4. Be respectful. *Not so much.*
5. Make the customer's experience a happy one. *Are you kidding?*

But no problem. My heart was still full of goodwill.

As we left Jackson Hole three days later, the splendor that had greeted our group with so much hope upon our arrival got smaller and smaller in the rearview mirror, then faded from view altogether. Not one of us had a book contract in hand, but the Being who created the magnificence that surrounded us bore gifts just the same. I'm not just talking about the carefree camaraderie, the tranquil lakes and radiant mountain peaks, nor the moose and its baby that crossed the road right in front of us.

No, what we treasured almost as much was the gift we had wished for in the first place: an agreeable stay at a comfortable Wyoming hotel. Stacy had eased up on her tough talk, and we ended our visit problem-free in the smaller room—the one that had two real beds, air conditioning, a working telephone, no nightlife noise, and yes, toilet paper in a dry place.

True luxury at half the price.

Our reward for having goodwill in our hearts.

Roosters and Honey Buckets

"Let's see . . . there's Wendy's," drawled the man who was required by Oregon law to pump my gas. "And o'course you got yer McDonald's."

As an out-of-towner passing through on a road trip, I was seeking his recommendation for a restaurant people raved about.

"Then there's Roosters. Over there." He pointed across the highway to a gigantic chicken, easily the highest structure in all of Pendleton, Oregon.

"Yep. Roosters. I go there a lot." He wiped the grease from his hands onto his overalls.

Wary, to say the least, we headed for Roosters. I *had* asked for one people raved about. I had to trust him.

What a pleasant surprise. Not only was it charming—decorated like a playful barn inside—but I had the best Asian chicken salad I'd ever had. Ever.

As the luscious combination of flavors and textures exploded in my mouth, memories of a search for another eatery, years before, came to mind.

It was like this.

We were four, spending a day in Seattle before heading to Canada for a weeklong survival camp. It was early evening, and our plan was to take a Duck Boat tour, then have dinner.

At the foot of the looming Space Needle sat the Duck Boat ticket shack. As I waited in line, I glanced to my right and saw six women simultaneously exiting a bank of royal-blue port-o-potties—all of them wearing duck-head hats, all of them glancing side to side, giggling at the coincidence that they had finished up their business at exactly the same time. I winced. *Hope they're not on our tour.*

Fascinated by the idea of a Duck Boat leaving the water and immediately turning into a Duck Van to take us through the streets of Seattle, I excitedly approached the booth.

"Sorry, ma'am" said the Duck Man. "Sold out. Try again tomorrow."

"Oh, no," I moaned. "Well, let me ask you: is there a restaurant around here that people rave about?"

He didn't hesitate. "Yeah, Honey Buckets. Over there." He waved his handful of bills in the general direction of Over There.

"Okay," I instructed my friends. "Look for Honey Buckets. The man said it's a popular restaurant in Seattle." Images of succulent menu items rose in my mind. *Mmmmm. Honey Buckets.*

Off we went. Four pairs of eyes saw nothing on our block. Nor on the next. Nor the next.

So we changed directions and headed toward what appeared to be a parade. Lawn chairs lined the streets, police officers patrolled the crowd. I scanned the mob to see if, by chance, some of the spectators were eating food-to-go from this elusive restaurant that everybody raved about. Maybe someone with a crinkly bag bearing the golden words "Honey Buckets," someone who could direct us to the source of the mother lode.

No one.

"Let's spread out and ask directions," I proposed.

I approached the nearest policeman. "Sir, I'm looking for Honey Buckets. Could you tell me where it is?"

"No idea, sorry. I'm not from around here; I'm just working the parade tonight. What's Honey Buckets?"

"It's a restaurant," I informed the officer. "Someone said it's a place people rave about."

"Sorry. But it sounds good—I'll have to try it sometime."

With four of us interrogating the locals, I kept hearing the words "Honey Buckets?" popping up throughout the throngs like—well, like donut holes in hot oil. Man, was I hungry.

Fifteen minutes later, we all reconvened near the Duck Boats. No one had known where Honey Buckets was, although almost everyone we'd asked said it sounded familiar.

This was weird. How could people in Seattle not know how to find their most popular restaurant? And a restaurant that was so close by, at that?

By now, my hunger pangs had become ferocious. Visions of beefy burgers, lettuce wraps, jumbo shrimp, fajitas overflowing with spicy peppers and strips of chicken, crisp salads and colorful steamed vegetables stormed my imagination.

I had worked myself into a Honey Buckets frenzy.

"I might have seen it when we were walking from the car," one of our group finally remembered.

About-face. Back we trudged toward the car.

Suddenly, another friend shouted, "Honey Buckets!"

The other three heads jerked in the direction she was pointing, desperate to eye our coveted Honey Buckets, counting the seconds until we could satiate our now-voracious appetites.

We followed our leader to the elusive pot at the end of the restaurant rainbow.

And gasped.

There in front of us stood a row of bright-blue port-o-potties—inscribed with the words HONEY BUCKETS.

Alas, a simple case of mistaken identity.

The Duck Boat vendor apparently thought I was seeking a rest*room* that people raved about.

Honey Buckets of Seattle.

Believe me, it was no Roosters.

My Secret Recipe

A version of this essay appeared in the December 2014 edition of Business Heroine Magazine *(businessheroinemagazine.com)*

Long before my favorite cookbook was smudged with oil, caked with flour, and stained with seasonings, I learned how to make cinnamon rolls. After tweaking my original recipe over the decades, I now serve huge, flaky, buttery blocks of golden dough, swirled with cinnamon and sugar that rival anything the Cordon Bleu could create.

Everyone says they're the best cinnamon rolls they've ever tasted.

But it was a long time coming.

The holidays were approaching in Southern California in 1971. Newly married and two thousand miles from my Midwest home, I craved snowy days and lighted pine trees.

Instead, it was seventy and sunny on the San Pedro side of the Palos Verdes Peninsula, and colored lights winked from rows of palm trees, trying to seduce me into this foreign setting. But I wasn't buying it. Christmas just wasn't Christmas without flurries, firs, and fires in the hearth.

I had to do something to save Christmas. *What*, I wondered, *would fill this apartment with at least a semblance of yuletide magic?*

Enter the Betty Crocker cookbook.

My tentative, newlywed fingers thumbed through the pages and eventually stumbled on cinnamon rolls. *Hmm*, thought I. *Could I possibly?*

Fumbling through my kitchen, I managed to gather enough wedding-gift bowls, pans, and measuring cups to start the project, and away I went. Soon, the scent of yeast wafted through the kitchen as the dough rose to new heights. A little punching, slicing, smearing, and sprinkling later, and my treasures were ready for the fire.

By the time my graduate-student husband came home, our apartment on Eighth Street was filled with the warm, sweet aroma of my first batch of cinnamon rolls.

"Well, do you like them?" I asked when he'd finished his treat.

"Sure," he replied. He brushed the crumbs from his shirt and gulped the last of his Yuban coffee. "Yeah, they're good."

"So . . . would you say they're the best you've ever tasted?" I teased.

"Of course."

Little did I know that the legend of my cinnamon rolls was about to take on a life of its own.

A few weeks later, we had friends over for brunch, so once again I made my pastries.

"*Someone* told me these are the best cinnamon rolls they've ever had," I enticed them, waving the pan of hot goodies past their noses.

"They are! They are!" was the group response.

So now I had the endorsement of more than one person.

The next time I punched and rolled that dough, I had my line ready.

"*People* say these are the best cinnamon rolls in the world." Might as well put it out there.

"I would agree," said one, then another, then another, until everyone in the room had felt sufficiently pressured to concur.

The years rolled on. Although I had learned to make those monsters quite well at sea level, when we moved from California to Colorado, an increase of 5,280 feet in altitude caused my masterpieces to turn out as hard as rocks. Since there was no Google yet, I called Colorado State University's practical-matters-help-hotline and found out I was supposed to decrease the amount of yeast at that high altitude. *That's all? Okay!*

I made a list of all our new acquaintances in Littleton and planned to wow them with my world-famous cinnamon rolls. Well, not world-famous. I hadn't actually taken my rolls overseas, so being a stickler for the truth, I left "world-famous" off the billing and stuck with what was factual: No one had ever said they *didn't* like my cinnamon rolls, and, in fact, when I cornered each guest who'd ever entered my house and asked if they thought these were the best cinnamon rolls they'd ever tasted, every single person had said yes.

With that, my very next cinnamon roll self-made testimony was this: "*Everyone* says they're the best cinnamon rolls they've ever tasted."

"Yes."

"Yes."

"Oh, yes."

"Definitely."

"Without a doubt."

It was settled.

Now, forty years later, everywhere I showcase my signature talent, I hear nothing but fervent agreement. They are simply the best cinnamon rolls anyone has ever had.

So there you go. I've just released a three-step, kitchen-tested recipe for getting compliments. It is this:

1. Make 'em big.
2. Serve 'em warm.
3. Come right out and ask your guests if they aren't the best they've ever tasted.

You have my permission to try it for yourself.

Inside Jokes

A version of this essay appeared in the March 2015 edition of Business Heroine Magazine *(businessheroinemagazine.com)*

One evening, when all my adult children were gathered for several days of Christmas celebration, Andrew stood up and posed a disconcerting question. "Hey, do you guys know if there's a vet open this late?"

Everyone glanced worriedly at Scully, his new pup. "Well, there's one not far from here. A veterinary emergency clinic," Betsy ventured. "Why?"

Andrew lowered his voice to a machismo bass and flexed his bulging biceps. "'Cause these pythons are SICK!"

Tim followed with his own variation: "Hey, is there a dog park around?" With a flexed arm: "'Cause these puppies are barking to get out of their cages!"

From that day on, obnoxious manly-muscle quips would pepper our conversations. Another inside joke was born.

Writer Dolores Curran, in her book *Traits of a Healthy Family*, interviewed dozens of professionals about what they see in well-adjusted families. At the top of the list: a sense of playfulness. Lucky for me, I've been treated to decades of humor and lighthearted bantering from my offspring, and I can say unequivocally that there's no one I would rather spend time with. It's always a party, and often those inside jokes are the entertainment. Whether it's from movie quotes misapplied, gag-worthy platitudes, or funny lines provided by small children, our playfulness thrives on inside jokes.

Take this one, for example: "You're just talking 'cause your mouth is moving" is one of our family's frequent quips. This dates back to 1972 when I watched my brother haggle at a market in Tijuana, Mexico—just for the sake of haggling. After about ten minutes, the exasperated vendor finally spewed his ammunition: "Go away! You're just talking 'cause your mouth is moving." So whenever one of us gets too opinionated and won't let it go, we have our line ready.

Another came from a family friend. Frazzled after her yoga studio increased her schedule to an unmanageable level, she finally announced she needed to either cut down or resign, or she wouldn't survive. But instead of proposing a pragmatic solution to keep her on board while supporting her in her attempt to take care of herself, the owner fed her a line of gobbledygook: "Now, slow down. I think you just need to ground to the Source, spend some time meditating—and I'll see you at the next class." So in our family, "just ground to the Source" is our solution to any dilemma that comes up.

And this one came from the years when my young children exhibited selective hearing. Their distractedness caused me to make such statements as "I put your boots in the front closet. Where did I put your boots?" Their answers assured me that they had heard me, and the tactic always worked. But that boot is on the other foot now. It's reached the point where they know how lost in thought I can get, so now it's "Mom, I'm putting your address book on the shelf below the phone. Where am I putting your address book?" And I'm required to answer.

Children, in fact, are a great source of inside jokes. My daughter Betsy, for example, gave our family the perfect word for those ubiquitous, pesky stink bombs when she announced one day with intuitive onomatopoeia: "Oops! I zipped." Of course, that didn't stop a certain unnamed son from using the "potty language" version he had learned from his little buddies. It seemed nearly incurable until I came up with an appropriate training tool: he would be confined to the bathroom, with the door closed, where he would have to shout the unsavory word at the top of his lungs ten times. He hated doing it so much that it put an end to his distasteful language. "Get into the bathroom" has since been our family joke whenever someone emits a swear word.

That same son gave us another inside joke when, as a young adult, he said something a tad objectionable, and followed it immediately with, "I'm sorry, Mom. You raised me better than that." That line has reverberated through the years by nearly every family member. Even I've had to resort to it a time or two ("Sorry, kids. You raised me better than that.")

Playfulness belongs in a home. Laughter can heal the heart and lift the spirit to create a haven of safety and comfort faster than anything else. I can think of no better way to ground to the Source than to establish inside jokes and live playfully ever after.

For a sampling of charming childhood quotes that can easily turn into a family inside joke, check out the entertaining website Quippsy: http://www.quippsy.com.

Jet Setter

My purple suitcase sat at the foot of my bed, its mouth gaping in anticipation of all the goodies I would throw in. Toothbrush. Toothpaste. Deodorant. Clean underwear. Vitamins. Check.

Those were always the most important to me. Having perfected the art of living minimally while traveling, packing clothes was more of an afterthought.

As the mother of an airline pilot, I had privileges I'd never dreamed possible: free travel anywhere in the world, and cheap buddy passes for friends and extended family. But being a humble family of modest means and simple lifestyle, trips back to Minnesota every couple of years to see relatives and short stays in the mountains had always been travel for us. So we should never have been living like this.

Like jet setters.

Yet there we were, various combinations of family members at various times enjoying trips to Switzerland, France, Germany, England, Ireland, Asia, Costa Rica, and New Zealand. One-day trips within the country were even more commonplace. At a moment's notice, I once flew to Minneapolis—just for the day—to take my mom out to lunch on Mother's Day. On another occasion, I flew to Oakland, California, where my daughter Anne was living. And then there was the time I set up a Saturday lunch date with my childhood best friend in Seattle. I caught a ten a.m. flight, landed in Seattle, had lunch, walked the beach, and was back home in Denver by evening.

But the trip that made the biggest impression on me was the one I was about to take: to Philadelphia to bring my son Andrew his Easter basket. It was his first year in college, meaning first year on his own, and I thought he needed a concrete reminder of home.

I zipped up my suitcase, grabbed the twelve-inch-tall, oval-shaped, green wicker egg loaded with Andrew's favorite candies, and hauled it all to the car.

I had a good plan. I had noticed that any flight I took out of Denver would land me in Philly late in the afternoon. But I didn't plan to spend a night there, so I had to figure out how to get there in enough time to spend a solid day of quality time with my son, and still get home. A redeye flight would work, but from Denver, that wasn't an option.

I had to think outside the box.

Checking the flight schedule on my computer, I found the perfect solution: I would leave Denver at 7:00 p.m. and head west to San Francisco, arriving at 8:45 p.m. At 11:00 p.m., I would board another flight from San Francisco to Philadelphia, arriving at 6:00 a.m. Brilliant. I would get a good night's sleep on the plane and be ready for a day of fun with Andrew back East.

It worked like a charm.

But to illustrate how small the world had become through this jet setting lifestyle, let me tell you the funny part.

I got off the plane in San Francisco, checked the flight monitor, and proceeded to walk to the next gate to wait for my Philly-bound flight. Ready for East Coast cold, I was bundled up in my black wool coat, scarf, hat, gloves, and boots. Dressed like that in California, I figured I'd stand out, but I had opted to wear my winter gear instead of carrying it since I was already juggling my suitcase and the gigantic, egg-shaped Easter basket I was determined to deliver.

Stand out I did, apparently, because as I focused intently on balancing that delicate basket on my suitcase, hoping I could get it to Andrew in one piece, a tentative voice suddenly broke my concentration.

"Mom? Is that you?"

I looked up without any sense of surprise. For years, I, as a lot of mothers will also admit, often assumed any "Mom" I heard was directed at me, even if it wasn't.

But this time it was. The owner of the voice walked up to me, craning her neck. "What are *you* doing here?" There stood my daughter Anne and her boyfriend.

"I'm delivering Andrew's Easter basket," I responded as if we had just met on the sidewalk and Andrew lived two doors down.

"But he's in Philadelphia," she informed me. "That's in the other direction." I detected a real concern for my sanity in her voice.

And then the curiousness of it all struck me. "What are you doing here?" I asked.

She looked at me like I had really lost it. "I live here, Mom."

"You live in Oakland. I mean what are you doing at the San Francisco airport?"

Turns out she and her boyfriend were there to pick up a friend from Denver, who was coming to visit. Had I known, I told her, I would have brought a couple of extra Easter baskets.

Believe it or not, the utter coincidence of this didn't strike me until much later. A fluke, yes, but not an earthshaking one.

Those are just the things that happen when you're a jet setter.

Third Glass
UNDERAGED

Underaged

Fat snowflakes flew across the sky in diagonal sheets like frenetic shoppers descending on Presidents' Day sales. With drifts up to four feet high blocking the roads, it was a snow day for the children. The usual get-up-for-school groans and pull-the-blankets-over-the-head drudgery were instantly replaced by effervescent whoops and energetic leaps down the stairs.

"What should we do today?" echoed five voices throughout the house.

The usual activities ensued: some television, a few board games and Lego competitions, a little make-believe. Then the boredom set in.

That's when I brought out the kids' funny books.

What had started out ten years earlier as language record books, at the suggestion of a preschool teacher, in which parents could record their children's language as it developed, had soon turned into a tome of quips the children had made in their innocence. Quotes grew into vignettes and, from one child's proud announcement that her January birthday was "wary-wary tenth" to another's demand that he be allowed to wear his "chocolate socks," I had a treasured history of their little-kid personalities, preserved forever in a collection of spiral notebooks.

The kids loved them. We spent hours that blizzard-filled day, each child reading his or her quotes and stories to the others, all laughing louder than they ever did while watching TV. Their own narratives were their Chardonnay.

Ah, children.

Kids are natural wellsprings of joy, fun and laughter, exploration, adventure, and complete abandon. As American poet William Stafford said, "Kids: they dance before they learn there is anything that isn't music." With children as our role models, who needs wine? Indeed, they'll dance through life with their inborn Maypoles of buoyancy, unaware that they should be anything but the age they are.

Which is why we enjoy them so much, why we laugh with them in giddy solidarity. And which is why it's so hard to see them scared. Or hurt. Or shamed.

MAGGIE McCANN PIKE

This collection of stories about kids—the underaged—represents the natural humor, honesty, and resilience that spring from their genuineness, their obliviousness, their complete lack of self-consciousness.

Kids are so refreshing, aren't they?

Bartley

I would like you to meet Bartley. Bart is a third-grader I tutor, who is totally uninhibited and usually arrives with a million stories to share, so as to delay his tutoring. A little tree trunk of a boy, he has a Charlie-Brown-wide face, thick, dark hair, and mud-puddle eyes that glow with excitement and sincerity. I love him to death.

He arrives this morning and, hands waving and neck craning, launches into a nonstop monologue, which he often does. I have my notebook on my lap, and I'm furiously writing what he says, for fear you won't believe this all came from one child. It did.

"I might have lice. They told my class it's all over the school. But it started with the big kids. Someone had lice and it got all over the place. What *is* lice? But guess what? We have a 'Beware of Dog' sign in our yard. Hmm . . . I . . . just . . . realized. We should take it down 'cause I'm not scared of my dog anymore. By the way, my little brother likes to go to after-school daycare because he sort of has a girlfriend there. But he's gotta get over her 'cause he's already in kindergarten and she goes to a different school. My dad went to a school where lawyers go only they aren't really lawyers. Do you know what that is? It has a name, but I don't remember. But me and my brother go to the best school in the county. We have the best teachers and guess what? They *picked* the best teachers for our school. Only nobody knows it. But the principal told us that, so that's how I know.

"And you know what's a coincidence? My class is having buddies with my first-grade teacher. She was mean to me. Well, I *was* a little hyper back then. I'm scared to see her 'cause I think she's still mad at me. But . . . I guess I just have to keep my cool, stay calm, and I'll be okay. What do lice look like?

"And by the way, I've played a *lot* of sports in my life. But I never got hurt. I got hurt when I closed the car door and forgot to take my finger out. Did you read *Diary of a Wimpy Kid?* It's all out of order. It's like a mixed-up hamburger with the pickles where the hamburger goes and the lettuce where the mustard goes and no bun on the bottom but two buns on the top. It's a crazy book. And besides, I don't understand the weather in

Colorado. In the a.m. it's all sunny, and then in the FM, all the clouds roll in. It's crazy.

"That reminds me. I saw two words in a book and they both started with A, but in 'apron' the A said 'eh,' but in 'adopt' the A said 'uh,' and I told my teacher, 'Whoa. It's like the world is upside down for me right now. I feel like I've been invited to a girl's party.'

"By the way, you know what? We don't even have our Halloween costumes yet. We're way behind schedule. The countdowns are ticking. Literally. Are the lice's eggs hard or soft? Can we google it? And you know what? I'm going to try not to fart this year at the Halloween party. Sometimes I just can't help it. My bottom starts to jiggle, and then it jiggles and jiggles till I just can't stop it. That happened to me last year at the Halloween party at the rec center. Phew. That was one short party. Everyone left. Fast. Even the teenagers couldn't take it."

And with that, Bartley and I get to work.

Flash Mobs for Safety

This vignette was published as a guest commentary in the Denver Post *on November 25, 2012*

Four of us shared dinner last week, three of us mothers, one a devoted aunt. The topic of the *Denver Post*'s epic series on child abuse and neglect in Colorado shifted our uplifting, complacent conversation.

"I just couldn't read it," said one. "It's more than my psyche can handle."

Shoulders slumped at the dinner table, each of us feeling powerless to solve this enormous problem. If social workers themselves feel defeated in their attempt to save children, what could *we* ever do?

My mind drifted to a young man I had met who himself had been abused. "You know what I do when I see a parent mishandling their child?" he had asked me. "I offer him a stick of gum. Catches him off guard. It's a nonviolent way of letting him know someone's watching."

Sadly, less than two weeks later, I was able to use that advice. I was walking my dog, Kalu, just a block from my house when I heard loud shouting from a nearby porch. A toddler was having a fit, and her mother's rage was rising by the minute. Then the dad came out and added his own berating, the child growing more and more distressed. *Drat. No gum.* Afraid they were getting close to striking, I sprang into action. I marched across the street and stood right in front of their house, staring them down. And then I pulled out my "gum": Kalu.

"Would she like to pet my dog?" I asked as I walked onto the grass.

The parents looked up, surprised. Gradually, the tone softened once they took a break from their tirade.

The mother bent down and scooped up her child. "Wanna see the puppy, sweetie? Oh, you're so tired, aren't you?" She sat down on the porch swing and cradled her daughter. Dad hovered, too.

Was this for my benefit? Of course. I worried about what happened to that girl every day thereafter when no one was around. But for a brief moment a child didn't get swatted. A little girl heard loving words, felt her mother's arms embrace her.

A short time later, I took part in a spectacular intervention. It was dusk, and I was walking to my car outside my local supermarket. Suddenly, a sharp screech pierced the air. "Get over here, you f@!% brat!" The child protested, but the mother only screamed louder. Then she yanked his arm and threw him into the car before reaching for the second child, fury warping her face.

My heart was pounding, but I planted myself in the middle of the parking lot and faced her dead-on, furtively slipping a package of gum from my purse. Soon, another customer got out of his car and positioned himself in plain view. Then two more appeared out of nowhere, like a Hallelujah flash mob. Within minutes, a posse of seven encircled this woman, each one of us ready to use whatever "gum" we had to rescue a child if needed. Not a word spoken among us, but it was clear this woman was not going to get away with hurting her children as long as we were around. Regrettably, we weren't able to change the core problem; all we could do was our best in that moment. And we did.

Talk of remaking our social service agencies to better protect our children abounds. But how about this: Can we gather together as humankind and serve as an important branch of protective services for kids?

We could start with the holidays. Parents will be crawling the malls—often with children who are tired, hungry, and bored, and who will behave as children do. We're going to witness frustration, anger, maybe outright abuse. Hidden among the throngs, though, are people like you and me. Flash mobs for safety, emerging en masse when needed.

All we have to do before leaving the house is make a list and check it twice: Wallet. Keys. Gum.

Let's roll.

Solomon Sarasin-Siskaroy

Solomon Sarasin-Siskaroy
A rollicking, riveting, misspoken boy,
As youngest of twelve,
He took on the task
Of naming those names
When someone would ask.
To say them he tried;
Really gave them a fight.
There was only one problem:
They'd not come out right,
'Cept, course, his own name,
The smallest young boy's,
Solomon Sarasin-Siskaroy's.
He couldn't say Yancy, but Yoyo was easy.
He tried to say Terrence, but out twaddled Tweezy.
He dubbed Barbara Bobby, Tanya was Toy,
And Bradley sounded a lot more like Boy.
He tripped over Georgie and stumbled on Joey;
They darted forth daftly as Dingle and Doey.
Mark became Markle
Charles, Chewy-Choy
He called Catherine Cawku
And Zebulon, Zoey.
At night as young Solomon knelt down to pray
His wee little voice could be heard to say,
"God bless
Yoyo, Tweezy, Bobby, and Boy,
Doey, Dingle, Markle, and Toy,
Cawku, Zoey, and Chewy-Choy—
And Solomon Sarasin-Siskaroy."

Misunderstood

Those who know me as an adult likely see me as a people-pleaser. But the journey from rule-breaking kid to law-abiding grown up was one that I undertook only after my strict parents had thoroughly housebroken me—a tedious process that took many years.

It wasn't that I was so naughty, I was just misunderstood.

My parents at times doled out housecleaning chores as punishment for deplorable deeds. Other times spankings, and whether they were by hand, with the hairbrush, or by means of the "Board of Education" someone had jokingly given my exacting trainers, I got more than my share.

My first chastisement came at age four. One day, my younger brother George and I made a stunning discovery.

"Georgie, come over here! Look!" I said. "Watch me." I reached into the ten-pound bag of sugar in the pantry and tossed a handful of the white crystals onto the linoleum kitchen floor. And I slid across that sugar patch.

George gave it a try. Then his eyebrows lifted as a brainstorm hit him.

"Oh! Oh! Watch this!" he said. He threw *two* handfuls of sugar onto the floor, took a running start, and flew across the room.

After that coup, we fed on each other's success. We learned that if we added a *lot* of sugar, we would soar across the kitchen like Olympic skiers in blue powder. So there we were, two preschoolers flinging by now the entire bag of sugar onto the floor, schussing forward, backward, and diagonally, while thinking we very well may have a patentable idea.

It didn't occur to me that our ear-splitting squeals might alert our mother.

So her sudden appearance in the doorway startled me. Without warning, there she was, eyes narrowed.

"I'll declare. What in the world are you two doing?" she asked, stunned.

"We . . . we're . . . just sliding," I tried to explain, sensing we might not be seeing eye to eye on this. George hid behind me, the coward.

Our mom gripped the broom and dustpan and pointed, wordless, to the living room where we knew she wanted us to go.

I still remember how I felt when we got busted: confused. Why would someone think something so fun was bad? Not only that, why didn't our mom want to join us?

As we got older and the crimes got worse, my parents got physical, in a 1950s sort of way. One time I was spanked for coming home late for dinner. Another time it was for yelling a word I had just heard at George, who had pushed me to my limits. And then there was "insolence," a word my mother used a lot, and which I understood at a very young age. Mom told me once that I was always rolling my eyes at her, which I was totally unaware of, so I most likely received a licking or two for being insolent on those occasions.

I was often baffled when punishment came my way. How could I know it was past dinnertime when I didn't have a watch? How could I stop rolling my eyes when I didn't even know I was doing it? How could I have known George was going to snitch on me for swearing at him?

I think the truth of the matter was I had become quite a source of entertainment for my siblings.

Like the time word got out that there would be a licking that evening.

Living room. Seven o'clock. Be there.

Sure enough, at the appointed time, Dad brought out the hard, plastic hairbrush and drew his arm back. I ran away, of course, so he grabbed my arm and tried again. I pulled my little body as far away from him as I could, effectively leading him in circles like a toy plane on a tether. I can still see the blurred but laughing faces of Cathy, George, Doug, Mary, and Therese whizzing past as I made the rotations, yelping and screeching for added drama.

Fortunately for me, punishments less physical eventually replaced spankings, perhaps with the advent of Dr. Benjamin Spock's child-rearing wisdom. Good thing—my rear was getting pretty sore.

It should be clear by now that I never *tried* to misbehave. I just had a way of stumbling obliviously into trouble. Despite how it sounds, I put a lot of effort into behaving myself. And believe me, trying so hard to please was exhausting.

Which is what was swirling through my psyche the night we had a babysitter named Tootie. Tootie's real name was Kathleen, and she was a stone-faced teenager who was a chip off the block of her dour German parents. That night, something got into me and I decided to talk back to Tootie and refuse to do what she said. This would be my only chance ever to be downright, genuinely naughty, and I wanted to see how it felt. I wouldn't give in, and the angrier Tootie got, the more I pushed. Soon my siblings joined in and before long, Tootie had a riot on her hands.

Suddenly her lips tightened, her eyes glared at us through her narrow, dark-framed fifties glasses, her pallid skin finally gaining some color right before her deep voice exploded, all but rattling the windows: "JUST GET TO BED, YOU BRATS!"

It was exhilarating.

I fell asleep that night very satisfied with myself.

The next day, of course, Mom called us all together, handed us mops and brooms, and put us to work for the next couple of hours.

But there's more.

One of our favorite thrills was to scare the elderly couple next door. Mr. and Mrs. K had taken advantage of the empty lot between their house and ours, and had built a new house *practically on top of ours*. So close, in fact, that all we could see out the window was their west wall—barely four feet away. During the summer, a few of us siblings and our friends would slink along the narrow space between the two houses, sidle up to Mr. and Mrs. K's window, peer in at the contented couple watching television, and knock as hard as we could on the glass, laughing uncontrollably as they nearly jumped out of their seats.

Within seconds we'd hear the earsplitting shriek of Mrs. K at the front door. "YOU KIDS GET OUTTA HERE!" she would blare at decibel levels that shocked the nervous system. Off we'd sprint, not stopping until our lungs burned and our sides ached. The adrenaline rush was addicting. So back we went the very next night, and a few more nights, too, to torment our defenseless neighbors. After the third or fourth time, our mother gathered us in the kitchen.

"Have you been scaring the Ks at night?" she asked, already knowing the answer. She extended the cleaning supplies, and by then we knew exactly what to do.

Or the time my parents got a call informing them that all the McCann kids had been up on the roof the night before. See, it was like this: Right outside my parents' bedroom, and deliciously accessible through the windows, was the lower part of the roof, the part that covered the screened-in porch. Mom and Dad weren't home that night, and had left Cathy and me in charge. And since Cathy, as usual, was holed up in her room reading, I was in charge. So I led the troops on an adventure. We all climbed out the window, made sure our tennis shoes gripped the shingles adequately, and at first crept, then sprinted, hopped, and leaped across the roof, releasing loud "SU-per-man!" shouts throughout the neighborhood.

You guessed it—brooms and mops the next morning.

My goals in life during childhood were simple: have fun, explore, speak the truth.

But my parents understood it differently. Let's just say they never needed to hire a housecleaner in those days.

Bartley Again

Bartley, my third-grade student who comes to me for tutoring, is back. By now, I'm learning to set a timer to limit his stream-of-consciousness insights that invariably begin our sessions.

Today, it's the topic of snapdragons that sets him whirling.

"Yes, I do know what snapdragons are. I don't know how to describe it, but I know my mom doesn't like them. We had a little . . . incident . . . with snapdragons. What? Oh, they're flowers? No, I didn't know that. I was thinking of dragons, the ones that snap at you.

"Oh my gosh, Miss Maggie. There's a coyote right outside the window! Look at him. You should call the Denver Zoo. Really. They'll come and get him from you and take him to the zoo. They *really* need some new animals there. Honest. Kids don't go there anymore. They don't think it's interesting. Basically, I saw a sign there last time that said, 'We're. Sorry. There. Aren't. Any. Coyotes. We. Couldn't. Catch. Any.' So they need some coyotes. I don't know their phone number. But wait! They probably have a website. You should check out their website. It's quick—like that!" He snaps his fingers.

"Actually, I'm not having such a well day. I got a paper cut all the way down my finger. Not the best part of my day.

"But my Dual Fusion shoes make me run so fast. But they're not in the top four. Kids Foot Locker lists the best shoes. Trust me. I checked the website and the top four are all Nikes. But my Dual Fusions grip, and all of a sudden I could run as fast as the fastest runners in my class.

"And guess what? My dad and I went to the Broncos and Steelers game. The Steelers fans were crazy. They were waving their towels all over and screaming and being crazy. Basically I wanted to flip my Broncos towel at those fans and knock some sense into them and say, 'Come ON. It's just a game.'

"But you should never slam your forehead against a robot. It really hurts. And besides, if you're really young you could get brain damage. But fortunately, I never got a fortune cookie that said, 'Bad. Luck. Is. Coming. Your. Way.' And my dad has a tax machine. Oh, sorry. It's a fax machine.

"I forgot to wear green last year on St. Patrick's Day. You should've seen me. Bruises all over my body from people pinching me. I finally hadda stack books up all around my desk to keep them away. That wasn't my best day.

"So that fire in Evergreen, did you see the smoke in the air? My mom says there hasn't been a fire that bad since *before I was born!* I'm sorry I didn't say hi when I first got here, but I had to hold my breath so I wouldn't breathe in smoke. It kinda felt like Earth was . . . a . . . a . . . a junk planet. It felt like that.

"And basically, I'm part Native American. That's probably why I'm so good at bows and arrows. I just feel like I know how to do it. Also, aiming. And shredding corn. Hey, my hands just go in the right direction."

The timer goes off. *Time to stop talking, Bartley.*

"Can I use your hand sanitizer?" Of course he gets the last word.

"Oooh. That feels smooth. It's just the feel of . . . clean. I never felt that before."

Now, let's read about those snapdragons.

Loaves and Fishes

As a child, I was mesmerized by all the talk about God in my Catholic schools, even if I sometimes got the theology wrong. Sometimes I tended to be rather literal. For example, toward the end of first grade, Sister Beatrice told us the scriptural story of the loaves and the fishes. It was magical to think of Jesus taking a couple of fish and some bread and changing them, without even a wand, into enough to feed thousands of people.

One day, Sister Beatrice made an announcement. "We're going to make a frieze, children. It will be all about the Bible stories we've read this year." I knew what a frieze was. She had used the word earlier that year when she taped long sheets of white paper across the blackboard and told us to draw on them. It had nothing to do with freezing, or going out in the snow, which I was glad about because I had left my mittens at home.

The classroom was electric with excitement as Sister Beatrice started handing out drawing assignments to various children, some in pairs, some by themselves.

"Margaret. Come over here, please. I would like you to draw the loaves and the fishes. This is your section of the frieze." She pointed to a three-foot empty space, put some crayons in my hand, and walked away. *Oh no.* I was used to being told exactly what to do. *How does she expect me to draw that?*

I waited for inspiration, then set to work. Being from the Land of 10,000 Lakes, and having an angler for a father, I had seen lots of fish. I drew one with every detail I could remember. Eyes, mouth, fins, tail, even scales. *Yep.* It was all there. Now I needed to draw some more. *How many fishes did Jesus have? And why do they say "fishes"? My dad just calls them fish.* I decided on the number five, then drew four more fish—one on top of the other.

Now for the bread. *Taystee Bread? Those loaves are rectangles. Or Wonder Bread, with its rounded tops? Those red, blue, and yellow circles on their packages are really pretty—maybe I'll draw Wonder Bread.*

For whatever reason—the Holy Ghost, maybe?—I ended up drawing hamburger buns. Again five, and again one on top of the other. I didn't end up drawing the Wonder Bread package they would have come in; I felt it was implied.

There.

Sister Beatrice came up behind me just as I was admiring my work.

"Hmm. That's not very good," she said, not softening her words one single bit.

She slid over to her desk, came back with a scissors, cut my part of the frieze out, and taped in a blank sheet of paper as I stood there speechless. "Mary Lou? Come over here, please, and draw the loaves and the fishes."

I wandered around the room not knowing what to do then. A half hour or so later, I glanced over at Mary Lou's drawing. She had sketched a tapestry of verdant, rolling hills, blue skies filled with flocks of birds, millions of little people drawn in perspective, and Jesus perched on a hill above them.

But it wasn't very good—she didn't even have any loaves or fishes in her picture.

The Burden of Boots

I happen to know that in 1950s St. Paul, Minnesota, the McCann kids were the only ones at St. Luke's Grade School who had to wear boots on rainy days. I know this because I would look at every single pair of feet on the playground, and every time I spotted some boots, my eyes drifted up those legs only to see a McCann attached to them.

The whole boot thing was an incredible source of embarrassment for me.

My brothers had it easy because their navy-blue corduroys, loosely secured with Roy Rogers belts, all but covered their boots. But the girls couldn't hide them. Dark-blue jumper . . . legs . . . boots. And these weren't charming polka-dotted rain boots or inconspicuous slip-on rubbers. No, they were the same slog-along boots we wore in the snow—thick, brown rubber, zipper up the front, fur trim around the top. Practical boots.

Every time it rained, I was filled with inordinate dread at having to look stand-out weird the next day at school.

So one drizzly night, I chased away my anxiety by concocting an elaborate plan.

It was eight p.m., and I lay awake in the double bed I shared with my sister, who was fast asleep. Slashes of rain on the window that looked out over the vacant lot below reflected onto the pink-flowered wallpaper inside.

I rubbed my hand along the thick, silky blanket that covered me. Normally I would have fallen asleep right away, but the nagging sound of rain kept me awake. Not because it was noisy, but because it tapped in me a foreboding of another dreaded Boots Day.

Why, oh why, do I have to look different?

And then the most glorious idea crept into my head.

I would get up at four in the morning, go outside, and spend two hours blotting up the sidewalks with dish towels. That way, my mother wouldn't know it had rained, and wouldn't make me wear boots. Two hours would be plenty of time to accomplish my mission before she woke up.

I crept over to my sister's bedside, quietly lifted the alarm clock off her end table, and clutched it to my chest as I scurried back to my side of the bed. After setting the alarm, I fell asleep visualizing how I would sneak past my parents' bedroom in the morning, conquer the creakiness of the stairs by tiptoeing on the outside of each step rather than in the middle, slither to the kitchen and grab the dishcloths, then escape out the front door to end the tyranny of boots forever. Or at least for the day.

Four o'clock came with a crash of thunder drowning the cacophony of the alarm. A gifted sleeper even at that age, it took me a few minutes to wake up enough to shut off the alarm. With only a modicum of consciousness, I could feel myself thrust into the battle between my urgent task and the beckoning, warm sheets.

At that moment, common sense woke up, snatched my body as it tried to haul itself out of bed, and threw me back into slumber.

Hours later, as I sat staring at my bowl of porridge, defeated, I held my hands to my ears at my mother's words: "Kids, don't forget your boots! We can't afford to replace shoes if they get wet."

Ten minutes later, I trudged up the street to my neighbor's house. Little Judy Fletcher needed someone older to walk her to school, so I picked her up on the way each day. When Judy saw me at the door, ghastly clodhoppers and all, she squealed, "Mommy! Can I wear boots, too? Pleeeease?"

Judy's mother was perplexed. "Boots? Why, I've put those away until next winter."

"Wellllll, I want boots, too!"

Reluctantly, Mrs. Fletcher headed down to the basement and brought up a pair of boots for Judy.

The breaking clouds allowed a timid slice of sunshine to cast its light on two little girls walking down Goodrich Avenue on their way to school that morning.

One of them was feeling proud she got to dress like her hero.

The other was just glad someone else was wearing boots, too.

The Day My Family Moved— Without Me

Spring had sprung full force. The rising sun cast its pink and gold streams on the duplex at 1455 Thomas Street in St. Paul, Minnesota. This was the fun time of year at school: field trips, picnics, and more coloring than normal—an easing up of the rigors of first grade as summer vacation approached.

I was enrolled at St. Columba's, a Catholic school with a church shaped like a ship. I thought my school was named after Christopher Columbus, and the church designed to resemble the Niña, the Pinta, or the Santa Maria, but then I found out Christopher Columbus was no saint at all, and that St. Columba was actually a medieval priest who guided his followers through several miraculous escapes from the sea and its monsters.

My mother seemed especially eager to send us out the door that morning. "Time to go," she announced. "Cathy, where's your jacket? Margaret, did you brush your teeth? George, slick down your hair with Suave." The brown bottle of greasy hair cream was a daily routine for the boys in the family.

Cathy, George, and I went next door to pick up Kathleen Lovenduski, and the four of us walked to St. Columba's together, then settled into our respective classrooms for another day of learning.

Three hours into the morning, Sister Beatrice announced lunch. We sat at our desks in our attention positions, that is, hands flat on the desks, forming Christmas trees with our forefingers and thumbs. At the signal, I headed into the cloakroom to grab my lunchbox. Mine was never hard to identify. My tasteful mother didn't stoop to metal boxes with Cinderella or Mickey Mouse guarding the peanut butter and jellies inside. No, she'd found something more refined for my sister and me: red-plaid, cloth bags with caramel-brown, leather trim and handles. More like purses.

But my lunchbox wasn't in the cloakroom.

Hmm. I guess I'm supposed to go home for lunch. I skipped over to the lunch-at-home group and trotted out the door.

It was eerie walking all by myself. *Where is Cathy? Where is anybody for that matter?* The street was deserted. To keep myself company until I got home, I decided to sing the song we girls performed every day at recess as we clapped our hands against each other's:

> I am a pretty little Dutch girl,
> As pretty as pretty can be be be,
> And all the boys on the baseball team
> Come chasing after me me me.
> My boyfriend's name is Tony,
> He comes from the land of Baloney,
> With freckles on his nose
> And twenty-six toes,
> And that's the way my story goes!

Fifteen minutes and fifty verses later, I was home. I ran up the front steps onto the porch and turned the door handle.

Locked.

I knocked on the door.

No answer.

Where is my mom? Why won't she let me in? I rang the doorbell. Jiggled the doorknob. Called out, "Mommy? Are you there? Let me in!"

Nothing.

Finally, I sidled over to the window and peered in. What I saw made my stomach roil.

Nothing.

There was no furniture at all. My house was completely empty.

I panicked. *Where did my family go? What should I do? I'm all alone.*

All alone.

The only thing I could think of was to go next door. A surprised Mrs. Lovenduski wiped her hands on the flowered apron covering her dress.

"Margaret! What are you doing here?"

"My mommy isn't home." I swallowed my tears. "I came home for lunch and she's not home and there's no furniture in my house." Mrs. Lovenduski's round face exuded sympathy.

"Oh, honey, your family moved away this morning."

A Chardonnay a Day

I felt sick. *Moved away? Without me?*

"Come in, dear. I'll make you lunch and you can go back to school. I'm sure your mother will pick you up after school." Mrs. Lovenduski handed me a glass of milk and a plate with a sandwich, an orange, and half a Milky Way. But I was too upset to eat. *Well, okay, I guess I could eat the Milky Way.* Down it went, one tiny bite at a time.

"I guess I'll go back to school now. Thank you for the nice time, Mrs. Lovenduski." My mother had insisted I say that to the mom whenever I left a friend's house.

"I'm sure everything will work out, dear."

I plodded back to St. Columba's, planning my future. *I could sleep in the cloakroom tonight, unless Sister Beatrice discovers me there. Maybe I could fit on a pew inside the ship-church. Or maybe go back to the Lovenduskis.*

One thing was certain: it was going to be a long, scary day.

I settled into my desk and got to work, nervously twisting my hair with my pencil. When the three o'clock bell rang, I was paralyzed in my seat.

Just then, my sister Cathy appeared at the classroom door, smiling and waving. "Over here! Come with me. Mom's waiting for us in the car. We get to go to the new house today."

I had never been that happy to see my sister in my whole life.

As we walked toward the car, Cathy shoved something into my arms.

"Oh, and here's your lunchbox. I was supposed to give it to you."

Pagan Babies

My third-grade religious formation at St. Luke's Grade School in St. Paul, Minnesota, was 1950s typical. The Baltimore Catechism had all the answers to everything, and so did we—because we memorized them verbatim. But there was also a social dimension to our training which mandated outreach to those less fortunate. Specifically, pagan babies.

We were all atwitter one Friday because Sister Patrick Mary had set aside an hour in the afternoon as Pagan Baby Day.

"Good news, children," she had announced. "We're going to buy a pagan baby."

Thirty-two third-graders exploded in cheer.

"I'm glad you're so happy. You know, pagan babies are very unhappy. These babies are born in parts of the world where they don't know about God. It's your duty as Catholic schoolchildren to support them financially. We'll do this on Friday."

Sister went on to explain that each of us would bring in money to pay for our pagan baby.

"You should work for your money, though. If you don't get an allowance, ask your parents if you can do some jobs to earn money. Sacrifice is important to your faith, children."

The brave ones moaned. I smiled and nodded.

"And then we'll choose a name for our little pagan."

Cheers across the rows.

Sister explained the routine. We would get to march around the classroom one time for every coin we put in the box.

This was going to be fun.

On the day of the Pagan Baby March, we could hardly concentrate until two o'clock arrived. When the time came, we stashed our homework into our plastic bags, sat at our desks with our hands folded, and waited for the activities to begin.

The first job at hand, of course, was to determine whether we could even afford a baby. Had we brought enough money? As soon as Sister put on the music, we all began to march. *Clink. Clink. Clink.* One by one, our nickels and dimes plopped into the jar as each child passed by. Most could only afford five or ten cents, so as soon as their coins were in the pot, they had to sit down, dampening the fun of the event way too soon. But I was smart. Never one to end a party before its time, I had brought ten pennies. So when most of the kids were back in their seats, I was only on my third round.

Kindhearted Sister Patrick Mary saw the dilemma. So she made a new rule.

"I think it would be fair to go around the room once for every cent you brought. For example, if you brought a nickel, how many times can you march?"

Sister Patrick Mary, always making a lesson of everything.

Out of their seats bounded the eager pagan baby marchers. It wouldn't wind down for another twenty minutes. But, of course, there always has to be a class kiss-up. After everyone had sat down, Gregory was still marching because he had brought fifty cents. *Probably lives on Summit,* I remember thinking. Summit Avenue was the Dutch elm-lined street where lush residences joined the Governor's mansion in a lavish display of opulence. The rest of us wanted to get to the naming of the baby, but there was Gregory, waltzing around the room for the twentieth time. *How long will it take him to make the next thirty laps?*

But common-sense Sister Patrick Mary finally called a halt to Gregory's one-man parade of devotion to the redemption of pagan babies.

"We're going to name our baby now, Gregory. Would you like to join us?"

Finally. First name and middle name went up for a vote. The names we came up with sounded like a combination of saints and Cabbage Patch dolls.

"Bernadette Catherine," suggested Catherine, inspired by Saint Bernadette's visions of Our Lady of Lourdes. And inspired by herself, too, apparently.

"Arthur Harry," shouted Peter, trying to honor both his grandfather and uncle in one go.

"Gladys Rose."

"Elizabeth Anne Therese Little Flower."

What?

"Christopher Christopher." Ellen thought she was being helpful by proposing a double dose of the saint who, legend told, carried the Christ Child across a dangerous river. She would have been devastated had she known that years later, Christopher would be taken off the overcrowded list of saints by the Church.

In the end, we named our pagan the alliterative Peter Paul. Sister Patrick Mary liked the name immediately and engaged us in a discussion of the power of Peter, the Rock upon which Jesus built His Church, and of Paul, who spread the Word like no other.

Yes, this was a strong name for a pagan boy.

It was also a candy bar, but we didn't think Sister Patrick Mary would know that.

Falsely Accused

Sixth-grader Connor came to tutoring with his head down. No friendly greeting, no eye contact. As he slunk down in his chair, I caught a glimpse of his tear-streaked face.

"You had a hard day," I said.

He nodded.

"Can I go to the bathroom?" he asked. I knew Connor. A bathroom break was his escape when tutoring got too intense. Today, life was too intense.

"Of course."

Clearly, Connor had been crying all the way over. So it took him a little while to get a handle on things in the privacy of the bathroom. Finally, the flush. Faucet on. A steady stream of water for several seconds. Faucet off. He was ready.

"Wanna talk about it, Connor?"

He shook his head.

"Okay, let's get started. We're going to read a story called 'The White House.' The comprehension strategy we'll use is main idea and supporting details. So, what do you already know about the White—"

"My teacher took my laptop away."

I leaned back in my chair and nodded. I was on sacred ground.

"She thought I was playing with a flight simulator. I wasn't. The icon for my flight simulator looks almost exactly the same as the Word icon. Same colors, same shape. I clicked on it by accident."

It should be known that Connor was a born pilot. Or airplane designer. He talked of nothing but. So having a flight simulator on his laptop sounded like vintage Connor.

His tears started anew. My tissue box finds good use in my tutoring business, but usually to capture nasal bacteria from those incessant childhood colds. Connor grabbed a tissue, wiped his eyes, blew his nose, and continued.

"I told her it was a mistake, but she said she's seen me before looking at planes during class."

He lifted his arms in dismay. "Hey, my screensaver is an airplane.

What can I say? I like airplanes. But that doesn't mean I'm doing something wrong."

His tears continued to flow.

Oh, the heartache of being a sixth-grade boy, I thought. *Too old to cry, but the tears won't stop. Supposed to be tough, but life knocks you down. Trying hard to make it seem like it doesn't matter, but wanting so much to please. What can I ever say to restore his sense of well-being?*

"You know, Connor, something like that happened to me once."

He kept his eyes glued to the floor.

I told him about the time my second-grade teacher accused me of chewing gum.

It was quiet work time, and I was busy filling in the blanks of my worksheet. I was a conscientious student. Suddenly, I—and the entire class—jumped at my teacher's raised voice: "Margaret, spit that gum out *this instant!*"

Since I was the only Margaret in that 1950s class of Mary Anns, Mary Kays, and Mary Beths, I looked up. Heads turned my way.

"I . . . I don't have gum in my mouth," I stammered.

"Oh, yes you do. I saw you chewing. Don't lie to me."

More heads. I could feel heat coloring my cheeks.

"No, I don't," I quietly insisted, aware that everyone was looking by now.

"Well, if it's not gum, then it's candy. Whatever it is, get rid of it."

"I don't have anything in my mouth," I pleaded one more time.

"We'll all just wait until you take that gum out of your mouth." She folded her arms.

What was I going to do? How could I get rid of something if there was nothing there? She wouldn't believe me, everyone was watching, and my mouth was empty. Well, maybe there were a few toast crumbs remaining from breakfast. Okay, okay—I had snuck out of the house without brushing my teeth. But gum or candy? I knew better. I would never break a school rule.

But now, I had no choice. I had to end this distressing standoff.

Slowly, I got out of my seat. I walked between the rows of desks to the front of the class, bent over the wastebasket, and pretended to take something out of my mouth.

My teacher stood, arms still folded, smiling in triumph as I made the long trek back to my seat.

I looked at Connor, who had stopped crying.

"You know what, Connor? That teacher ended up becoming a pretty famous children's writer. Even teachers who become famous can be wrong."

Connor was all ears by now.

"Did you ever tell her?" he asked, his dry eyes aglow with conspiracy.

"Actually, I did. I wrote her a letter and sent it to her through her publisher. I said, 'Just want you to know that I really didn't have gum in my mouth that day.'"

Connor laughed. "Did she write back?"

"No. But at least I finally got my say."

My student relaxed into his chair, chuckling to himself.

"So, the question is, Connor, were you playing with your flight simulator at school?"

"No!"

"Then your teacher was wrong. That's all there is to it."

Of course, knowing what I know from my years teaching middle school and high school, I felt obligated to add one tiny caveat: "And if you were, well, just don't do it again. But, of course, you said you weren't, and that's all I need to know."

Bartley Barges into Adolescence

Bartley arrives for tutoring and shakes the snow off his boots. I've described him before as a tree trunk of a kid with big mud-puddlicious eyes and a Charlie Brown head covered with thick, brown hair. Bartley's charm lies in his innocent expression, the craning of his neck as he talks, the frequent changes of tone, the wrinkles that line his forehead when he has something serious to say. He started with me in third grade and is now in fifth, so he's a little taller, a little leaner, but still unassuming. He immediately releases his stream of consciousness with barely a hello.

"Guess what? My mom says I have to go swimming—*again*—right after tutoring. I just went last night and I was sick when I got home, but it was just that I had to get my digestive system going again. I wasn't really sick, but I felt sick, so I just had to relax on the couch and watch TV. But she's making me go swimming again this morning. She says she wants me to get rid of my chubbiness. I said, 'Mo-om! It's just baby fat.' That's fat that gets on your stomach when you're about eight years old. It's about balance. Least I think it is. I used to not have baby fat and I had terrible balance. My friend Jack thinks he doesn't have baby fat. I told him, 'Yes you do, Jack. Our whole fifth-grade class has baby fat.'

"So my class had a puberty talk. They said we're stinky now and we gotta use deodorant and take showers. *Every* day. I mean, I use deodorant every day, sure, but I don't wanna take a shower every single day. Even the girls were told to use deodorant. Hmm . . . is that right? Do you think girls have to use deodorant? No, maybe they don't have to. We're the only class that's stinky at my school. But we're working on it. And speaking of deodorant, my mom got some for Christmas. The girl kind, with the holes on top. Not like the boys' kind that's solid. I like the dry kind. The wet one makes you feel like you got a bug crawling in your armpit. We even got my brother deodorant. He's starting to get stinky. He's almost seven.

"And speaking of emotions, you won't believe this: I was the last one standing in dodgeball. It was all the tough kids against *me*! Well, I learned this on a TV crime show: basically, you look the bad guy in the eye. It makes you look more fierce. So I did. And it worked. I was the *last one* standing. I just went in the bathroom and cried. But it was happy tears, don't worry."

I'm racing to keep up with Bartley as I scribble his words into my notes, my concentration causing a long pause on my part. He fills the silence.

"So. I got a lot going on in my life." He looks around the room, his thoughts still percolating.

"Oh, and I'm in the last stage of puberty now: mouthwash."

Oh, Bartley. Please don't ever grow up.

Freaked Out by Confirmation

It seems I've spent a lifetime trying to get this whole faith thing right. I've already told you about the pagan babies—those hapless infants born in parts of the world where Catholicism is not observed, to whom my classmates and I donated our allowances to "rescue" every year. But in fifth grade, it was time to start thinking about my own soul. It was time to receive the sacrament of Confirmation.

Sacraments are a beautiful concept, really. These rites are signs of God's presence and action in our lives, also known as grace. In this case, we would receive a special strength of the Holy Spirit in order to be true witnesses of Christ. Of course, I didn't understand that at the time, partly because we used the term "Holy Ghost" instead of "Holy Spirit."

That in itself was freaky enough for a ten-year-old.

But my biggest fear at that age had nothing to do with ghosts. No, my biggest fear was having to retrieve something from my basement when it was dark. Confirmation, I was told, was going to make me a "Soldier of Christ," which to me meant I would no longer be afraid to go downstairs after sunset.

I don't know why the basement scared me so much. It was, after all, where Queenie, our black Labrador, lived, and where she once even gave birth to a litter of puppies that my siblings and I stumbled upon by accident. We also regularly put on a variety of plays down there, lugging down every chair we could find for our audience of neighborhood kids, and using a bed sheet for a curtain.

During the day, the basement was a regular playground, but at night, in my vivid imagination, all manner of dangers lurked in that abyss, most based, assuredly, on Alfred Hitchcock episodes.

Now, with Confirmation looming, yet another fear arose: the archbishop. I had heard from my older sister that the archbishop would slap me to make sure I really was a Soldier of Christ.

Not only that, but my teacher had made it clear how important it was to know all of the Catechism answers, because the archbishop would randomly call on kids to recite them. The Baltimore Catechism was a book containing Catholic doctrine in question-and-answer form, graduating in complexity through the grades. We had started memorizing the Catechism in second grade, beginning with the question, "Who is God?"

I should clarify that my fifth-grade teacher was not the one who prepared us for Confirmation, because she was not a nun. Instead, Sister Leone came in each day to teach us Religion while Miss Flynn went to Sister Leone's room and taught something safe, like Geography. Sister Leone was the epitome of stern authority, and her caustic lectures convinced me that humiliation in front of the archbishop was a very real possibility.

Fourth- and fifth-graders were receiving the sacrament at the same time, so when the day of Confirmation arrived, my fourth-grade brother, George, and I walked to St. Luke's Church together. I shared my fears with George as we quickened our pace up Oxford Street toward the church on Summit Avenue, but he didn't seem to know what I was talking about. How he had missed the gospel truth about the terrors of our upcoming ritual was beyond me.

But I set him straight, and by the time we gathered with our classes in the basement of the church, I had George in near panic.

The ceremony was stately and majestic, with the archbishop standing in front, draped in his red cloak and miter, staff glittering. I joined the procession up the aisle, much as I had for my First Communion three years earlier, but this time, I was not smiling, for I was wiser in the matters of suffering for my faith.

The next two hours crawled by. I had several frightening trials to pass before the final anointing.

Trial one: the Catechism questions. The archbishop strolled closer to his young congregation and posed the first question.

"Who knows . . ." he began.

What? We had a choice *about whether or not to answer?* Hands shot up, but not mine. Not because I didn't know the answer, but because I tended to freeze whenever I had to speak in front of a group. A shortcoming, yes, but not necessarily an un-soldierly quality—I was hoping. I sank back into the comfort of my pew. First crisis over.

But now we would face trial two: The Slap.

Row by row, we were released to approach the altar, and because I was tall, I brought up the rear. I looked ahead and didn't see any reddened cheeks, nor anyone crying or doubled over in pain, but I figured that was because they were true Soldiers of Christ. When my turn came, I walked with resolve toward the rail separating the sanctuary from the rest of the church and waited my turn.

When the archbishop approached me, he held out his hand, rested it on my head, and proclaimed that I was a now a Soldier of Christ. Then he announced my chosen Confirmation name, which was my godmother's name, Monica, except he pronounced it with a Roman accent ("Mo-NEE-ka"). *How neat,* I thought. He then gently grazed my cheek with the back of his hand. *That's it? A mere stroke?*

Whew. Enormous relief.

Two down.

My final trial was waiting for me when I returned home: the bowels of the dreaded basement. As the sky got darker, a deep indigo blue replacing the bright spring heavens, I glanced nervously at the basement door. Yet I was consumed more by worry than fear.

What if Confirmation didn't take?

What if I fail this test and can't be a Soldier of Christ anymore?

Ever so slowly, I turned the knob. Guardedly, warily, I set my foot on the first step. *Oh dear God, my pounding heart.* Down I trudged, one step at a time, alarm boiling within.

Dang.

It was still there, that awful basement-terror. The sacrament of Confirmation had slid right off, like snow from a slanted roof during melting season.

That was my first crisis of faith.

Impoverished on Goodrich

How did it ever happen that a wholesome, "Minnesota-nice" girl, cradled in the arms of a strict Midwest Catholic family and raised in the classrooms of holy nuns, a girl whose parents and teachers pounded her with the mandate to conform, comply, and kowtow to the rules, how is it that such a girl got mixed up in the biggest corporate greeting card scandal St. Paul had ever seen, while becoming one of the city's most-wanted juvenile delinquents?

At the age of ten.

My best friend, Gianeen, and I were in fourth grade when, on a dreary November Saturday with no ideas for fun or excitement, we resorted to a game we played from time to time: thumbing through a magazine, each of us choosing which dress or car or advertised product we liked best.

But our game was interrupted right around page seventy-five, where a glossy ad called out to us. A greeting card company in Elmira, New York, was recruiting children from all over the country to sell their cards. According to the ad, they would send us the cards, and we would go around our neighborhood selling them door-to-door. Exciting, sure, but our eyes immediately skipped to the best part of the offer: just for signing up, the company would send us each a notebook and glittery pen—presumably for recording our sales—complete with a gold box to keep them in.

We were shoo-ins. And we had the sales experience to prove it: Each year, St. Luke's Grade School sent us out to fill our orange-and-black UNICEF banks with change while we were trick-or-treating. To put it modestly, Gianeen and I had brought back some pretty hefty funds for UNICEF'S humanitarian aid to mothers and children in developing countries.

As it turned out, the greeting card company didn't care at all about our sales experience; they just sent us the cards.

When my package arrived, I called Gianeen to bring hers over, too, so we could examine our eagerly awaited notepads together. The holder itself wasn't exactly crafted of lustrous gold, as it had appeared in the picture, but more like spray-painted plastic, and instead of high-end stationery, the paper was more like sticky notes, but without the sticky. The pen did work, however, and it *was* sparkly, so we had something worth showing off at school the next week.

An hour went by before we noticed the letter that accompanied the greeting cards. It explained the procedure for returning the profits once we sold all the cards. But we were more interested in the list of selling tips. For example, instead of saying, "Would you like to buy some cards?"—leaving the door wide open for a big, fat "no" from a prospect—we should say, "Which do you prefer?" Gianeen and I thought that was way too weird. We rolled our eyes and decided we would do it our own way. Besides, we already had our scratch pads and pens. At this point, we didn't really care how many cards we sold.

We stuffed the business papers back in the box, and off we went, up and down Goodrich Avenue, knocking on our neighbors' doors, appealing to their goodwill.

By the end of the week, Gianeen and I had grown weary of our new job. We'd sold a few boxes, and had each raised $1.20 for the New York company. But we didn't send in the money because by then we had lost the directions for doing so. More important to us was that we'd been able to wow all our friends at school with our glitzy notepads and pens. Talk about instant status. The two of us had started a fad in our class, passing around our little stacks of pages for autographs, which the other girls quickly followed. Our meteoric rise to adulation in Mrs. Powers' fourth grade class was just plain heady.

And then.

I don't know which one of us instigated the crime. I do know we didn't see it that way. It's funny how gentle the conscience can be sometimes. We were just hungry, okay? Those mini-jawbreakers in the turquoise box at Walter's Variety Store on Grand Avenue were only a nickel a box. And we had money—$1.20 each. I knew I could easily pay it back on Saturday when I got my weekly allowance of five cents for scrubbing the bathroom floor.

So down went the jawbreakers, keeping us entertained the rest of the day. The succulent balls of sugar, each in its own rainbow of layers—crimson turning orange, then yellow, then green, then blue, then indigo, then violet, and finally white—gratified us for hours as they slowly rolled around on our tongues, exploding like fireworks with one flavor after another.

Best nickel I ever spent.

But that first purchase with the card company's money turned out to be my gateway to hell, where the fires of preadolescent anxiety would rage, their ashes ready to bury my innocent soul.

Before I knew it, the entire $1.20 was gone, frittered away at the hands of impulse over several months. I was oblivious to the consequences at first. Letters began to appear in the mailbox—business letters postmarked Elmira, New York. They wanted their money. I knew I should be making an effort to recoup the funds, but week after week saw my allowance diverted to more pressing needs. I was unruffled, though: New York and Minnesota were many states apart. They'd never find me.

And then *the* letter arrived:

> We have turned your case over to our attorneys. You will be hearing from them.

Terror filled me. *Attorneys. That's serious.* Three houses down on Goodrich, Gianeen had received the same letter. The difference was that Gianeen actually told her parents, who immediately sent the remaining boxes of cards and a check for $1.20 to Elmira, New York, allowing their daughter to continue the life of a carefree ten-year-old girl. Not so with me. I couldn't bear to tell my parents what I had done, not in light of the scruples they had instilled in me.

The full burden of crime was on me. I would have to face this alone.

My life changed after that. I was on the lam. Visions of cops raiding my home and dragging me away in handcuffs taunted me mercilessly, day after day. Every time I saw a squad car drive down the street—looking for me, without a doubt—panic rose inside. My cheeks got hot, my stomach did flips, my breath raced. More than once, I ducked behind a shrub until my predator passed, or leaped into the enclosed front porch and crouched below the screens, or absconded to the backyard and buried myself in the overgrown lilac bush we kids used as a fort. They were relentless, those guys in New York.

My days as an outlaw began the summer after fourth grade and didn't stop until the end of seventh grade. Three long years of lost childhood, three long years of self-imposed impoverishment.

And then, liberation: My family moved—way across town. Far from Goodrich Avenue and the hounds of heaven that stalked me, I could at last leave behind my corporate scandal and my harrowing brush with the law.

And eventually, redemption: Once I got my first job as a teenager, I set aside $1.20 and placed it in the collection basket at church.

Alms for the poor.

Fourth Glass
PUNGENT

Pungent

Ever find that with a couple of sips of wine, you start to get quiet? Yeah, me neither.

In fact, the more relaxed I feel, the more profound I think I sound.

I get tongue-loose, at times downright pungent, mouthing off and spouting opinions about anything-and-everything-don't-even-get-me-started. Sometimes, needing an outlet, I even send my opinions off to the newspaper. That's the mild approach. Other times, I vicariously lash out—through other people's gutsiness. But once in a while, I'll erupt and call someone out; I take what's brewing inside and sling it onto the person who needs to hear it.

Believe me, I don't always feel better after an eruption.

So one New Year's Eve in my not-too-distant past, after I'd worn myself out with the tirades churning in my head, I made a resolution: "I'm going to stop having opinions." I said it out loud so I would hear it and hold myself accountable.

Suddenly, a cloak of peace draped over me.

Granted, political campaigns still polluted the airways.

But I have no opinion about that.

My homeowners' association raised its rates.

I have no opinion.

Wars continued, a new pope was elected, my strawberries from the health food store turned moldy in two days.

No opinion. None.

It was blissful, that state of complete detachment.

And then something unexpected happened: My opinions didn't go away. They slept obediently under the blanket of my will, but I could hear them stirring, trying to squirm out of their forced slumber. *Beliefs should be held but not heard? Hardly.* An occasional nap when they start to dominate never hurt anything, I suppose—things are fresher after a sleep—but they still scream to be heard.

My dormant opinions had resurfaced, only now they weren't as pungent as I'd once thought.

Isaac Asimov said, "Your assumptions are your windows on the world. Scrub them off every once in a while, or the light won't come in."

That's all I'd done—scrubbed them off.

What follows is a compilation of pungency: my own fervency coupled with the cheekiness of people I only wish I could emulate. Drink up.

Djangoed

This vignette was published as a guest commentary in the Denver Post *on February 24, 2013*

I have a hobby, which is to see all the "Best Picture" nominations before the Academy Awards. Most recently it was *Django Unchained*, the Quentin Tarantino film about a freed slave who becomes a bounty hunter and seeks to rescue his wife, still enslaved. I slipped into the theater knowing little else about the movie.

Before long, I could see there was a bit of spoofing going on. Bloodbaths permeated the plot, but it was clear the special effects crews had amused themselves by hurling vats of thick, red tomato sauce with each gunshot. Total hyperbole. Unrelenting carnage broke out from beginning to end, punctuated by lively dynamite explosions at the climax. I rolled my eyes and chuckled to myself.

It didn't help that Django and his dentist-turned-bounty-hunter mentor, Schultz, were riding in a stagecoach topped with a gigantic, bobbing tooth. Or that a posse of Klan-like stooges halted their raid to complain that their masks were so poorly made they couldn't see out of the holes, but who cared because what was important was that the horses could see. Or that Django's wife, Broomhilda, was trapped at Candieland, an ironically whimsical moniker for the mansion home of sadistic plantation owner Calvin Candie, where opulent, winding banisters slid chute-like up and down the ladders of antebellum social status. No child's play, this, but the funnies made the reality seem okay. For a while at least.

I was sitting in my seat, alternately giggling and gasping, easing back then clutching the armrest, because wrapped into all the satire was an increasingly dead-serious depiction of the real violence inflicted on slaves. Right in front of our eyes in graphic detail. The spaghetti in this western slowly wound into a sordid social commentary. I wasn't laughing anymore.

But what happened deep within me was the most disturbing part of the film. Ever so gradually, a seething grew that couldn't be contained. I was steaming with hatred. My fury begged for vindication—against the brutal oppressors who seared scars into the backs of slaves. Against Candie and the slave fights he staged in his parlor for sheer entertainment. Against head servant Stephen, who had taken on the worst qualities of his captors to keep his own brothers and sisters down.

Against evil incarnate.

The powerlessness that gripped me sought release. *Kill 'em!* I screamed inside. And with every spraying of bullets, I felt relief.

I was rooting for their deaths.

I wanted them off the face of the earth.

And then an unnerving thought intruded. I live midway between the "plantations" of Aurora, Colorado, and Columbine High School. In fact, at that moment I was in Aurora where, too recently, someone had let out a round of bullets in a theater much like this one, packed with people just looking for entertainment. For years, I taught in schools not unlike Columbine. Nationwide, more than one someone had stormed the halls of a school and brought down innocents, forever destroying innocence. So, too, do I go to malls, churches, public gatherings where political figures speak—all places where someone has inflicted violence. What were those thugs feeling when they let loose? At the moments of their massacres, were they also fueled by anger, powerlessness, a need to snuff out what they perceived as evil?

As I watched *Django*, I, too, could think of no other way to escape the chains of my wrath than to see those people dead. Do I actually share something in common with the worst of the worst?

I'm stunned by what I learned about myself, horrified that I could embrace violence to end violence, as I did throughout that movie. It disturbs me to think that for one moment, as I sought an end to the cruelty I saw on that screen, I might be of like mind with the shoot-'em-up guys.

That jangles my nerves. But I don't suppose Quentin Tarantino intended that.

Granny

The plump woman with white, Brillo-curly hair and the floral housedress was a fixture in our family photo album my whole life. I knew she was Granny, my mother's grandmother, and that she was strict during the years she lived with my mother's family.

But that's all she was to me: a woman in one dimension, a black-and-white glossy relative with no discernible personality.

Then one day, within a few hours, that one dimension blossomed into three, like one of those Magic Grow capsules that, when placed in water, suddenly becomes a foam animal. She was now Viola, mother bear, cafeteria worker, student of Unity, philosopher, risk taker, tobacco chewer. And, among relatives of a generation that was ashamed of cultural diversity, especially if it involved a darker complexion, Viola was—hush—the daughter of a "half-breed."

The reason Viola came alive for me: letters.

Stacks of Viola's erstwhile correspondence fell into my hands, some of them carefully written on parchment, others scrawled on lined school paper, but the pencil markings on all were faded from the years. Others were cards, exquisite works of art with colorful flowers raised in relief. Even a stack of newspaper clippings gave me insight into what was important to Granny.

The letters were communications between Viola and her family, uncensored and from the heart. One bore the signature of her husband, Joe, who wrote words of assurance to Viola (whom he called Mother) from a faraway hospital as he lay dying from mouth cancer:

> My Dear Sweet Mother,
>
> My mouth is very sore but will be well in about one more month. Won't that be good for us?
>
> From your Honey,
> Joe

It was his last letter.

There were letters to Viola from her children. "You must pull yourself together," wrote Maude, her eldest—my grandmother and the most flamboyant daughter—now softened by grief after Joe's death:

> I am grieved to death over Papa. It shocked me so, my sickness came on me for the first time and I am feeling just awfully bad. You must pull yourself together. You are all we have now, dear heart, so buck up, grit your teeth a little harder, and you will find after the first severe heartaches Daddy will be a sorrowful memory and a sweeter memory as the years go by.

In her letter to Viola, my Grandma Maudie moved into a spiritual place I hadn't witnessed in my times with her. Surely she was reflecting the religious upbringing Viola had provided her:

> Try to relax and let God and time bring the sweetness of life back to you. Just remember the same God that is watching over us is the one that has taken Daddy's poor old pain and trouble burdened soul home to rest and you should thank God for the mercy he has bestowed upon Daddy.

There was a letter to a medical professional. Granny's grit came through loud and clear in her response to the doctor who dared suggest she sell land to pay her grown son Bart's hospital bill of almost three hundred dollars. Bart had an abscessed kidney, which needed surgery, but darned if she was going to pay. "What in the world made you think I was responsible for this young man's bills?" she railed. "He is 30 years of age, and for years has ignored my existence. Write this boy yourself!"

And a letter that flaunted Granny's philosopher hat. At age fifty-three, she wrote about "something that has been worrying my mind for better than 10 years." Saddened by the loss of her family circle as the children left home, she concluded:

> The I that writes this is not the young woman that tended those children. They are all dead, as the past in which they live. I think if more mothers understood this it would ease the heart aches and longing and misunderstanding—that is the lot of the human mother.

Soon I found myself searching the letters for any signs of scandal in Granny's life, and a couple of times I almost found some. "I've been so sick," wrote Granny, "that I haven't been able to work but now I'm ready to kick the children . . ."

Oh no! She lived with my young mother and aunts. What did she do to them?

". . . are doing fine they're all back in school . . ."

Whew. The missing period after "kick" had transformed Granny from noble survivor to child abuser before I caught it.

"I've done a terrible thing," began another letter. I arched my eyebrows. "I haven't been faithful . . ."

Good, here it comes!

". . . about writing to you regularly."

Rats.

No ignominy anywhere. All I found in that box of letters was ordinary life as Granny had lived it in the late 1800s and early 1900s. But it captivated me.

Without Granny's notes, I'd never have known about her daily ritual of chewing tobacco. Or about the day when, bone tired from working in the cafeteria seven days a week, she just up and quit her job to spend the summer traveling. I'd never have known that I'm of Native American descent (a fact I value, but a guarded piece of information that "we don't talk about").

And just knowing that I'm much more like my peppy, adventurous great-grandmother than I am my own demure, conservative, reserved mother—that I'm not an anomaly after all—brought me great relief.

I rue the demise of letter writing. How will our descendants come to know us? Finding Granny's letters made me realize that what seems ordinary and unimportant right now will one day be a trove of immeasurable wealth to someone, and it's worth our time to write it down. I left my treasure hunt more determined than ever to make sure my stories reach the next generations—if not by letters, then by e-mails, by journaling, or just by talking.

But if I ever do take up the habit, I think that I, unlike Granny, will hide my chewing tobacco.

Sit at the Cat's Table

This essay was published in the April 2015 edition of Business Heroine Magazine *(businessheroinemagazine.com)*

Back in the 1960s, my high school boyfriend, Paul, surprised me with an enticing date: dinner at the Radisson Hotel in Minneapolis, where a violin ensemble, the Golden Strings, would serenade us. It sounded so romantic. When we got there, the waiter escorted us straight to our table—right next to the kitchen. The pure sounds of violins were drowned out by the cacophony of slamming drawers and screeching voices.

Come to find out, Paul and I had been assigned to the Cat's Table, a German term for the least privileged location at a banquet. Our shortcoming: we were teenagers.

Author Michael Ondaatje thought "Cat's Table" had a similar ring to "Captain's Table," so he wrote a book bearing that old German moniker. *The Cat's Table* follows young Michael and two other boys traveling on a ship from Ceylon to London in 1954. Like Paul and I, the boys, along with several "insignificant" adults, had been relegated to the Cat's Table, as far from the Captain's Table as possible. As you might have guessed, the story goes on to reveal that the "Golden Insignificants," as Ondaatje calls them, were far from trivial—they were pure gold. Michael's three-week voyage set him up with the gift of a lifetime: "It would always be strangers like them, at the various Cat's Tables of my life, who would alter me."

Assigning and denying people status seems to be part of the human condition. We've finally put safeguards in place, such as zero tolerance for bullying and nondiscrimination policies, but here's the problem: We can't control what we don't see. No parent, teacher, or boss can catch every word etched in a note, every whispered vitriol, every cruel glance. If the "sticks and stones" defense were really effective, we wouldn't have organizations promising that "It Gets Better."

I propose we make it better *right now*. And I know just how you can do your part: resolve to sit at the Cat's Table.

The Cats are those people you wouldn't ordinarily invite to your feast, for whatever reason. They are Ondaatje's Golden Insignificants.

Golden Insignificants are as diverse as their beholders. Yours might be the recluse in the office, or the obnoxious one who talks too loud, too much, too often. She may be the classmate with a disability that makes you uncomfortable. The colleague with a tic, body odor, or skin condition.

Humble people may be easier to befriend, but arrogant people can be Golden Insignificants, too. They polish their exteriors to perfection, but deep down fear they are inadequate. Your Golden Insignificant might be the charismatic woman, man, or child who, it appears, doesn't need any more friends. They are those who seem to have it all together. They may intimidate you, making it hard to see that underneath the attractive veneer is someone just like the rest of us, someone who craves a genuine friendship with a person who likes and accepts all their dimensions, not just the glamour. They would love to sit at your table.

Golden Insignificants are even people who are cruel to you and don't deserve your time. Invite them to your table. Make it your goal to dig beneath the egotism, the condescension, the conceit, and find the gold.

Your Cat's Table has room for a varied group. The local celebrity, the class president, the loner. The overconfident, the under-confident. The mainstream, the unique.

In truth, we're all Insignificants to someone. But everyone is a *Golden* Insignificant, everyone is a cache of beauty.

I can only imagine the impact a sit-at-the-Cat's-Table way of life would have on our world. There isn't a person on this planet who doesn't have luster beneath the surface. It's our loss not to enjoy that beauty.

So go ahead, grab a seat next to someone with whom you wouldn't ordinarily associate. If every day someone invited another to the Cat's Table, every day someone's life would change.

Splash Party

"So, going to your splash party, are you?" said my friend Gerry's husband, Jerry. Gerry—she—and I are water aerobics friends. Apparently, Jerry—he—thinks what we do is a little . . . foo-foo. Languid. Sluggish.

I'll admit I was once a bit of a swimming snob myself. I'd show up at the occasional morning class and leave feeling so far above those gray heads who shuffled in with their oxygen tanks and walkers, tossed the word "surgery" back and forth like a beach ball for an entire hour, and talked so much they couldn't even hear the instructor. *Time to join the evening class*, I'd tell myself. *Those are the driven exercisers, the ones working off the stress of their days, of their lives, with the energy of Olympic athletes. That's where I belong.*

But once I retired, I got to know the folks in the morning class, and what I learned has put me to shame. People who see heads bobbing in swimming pools across America and dismiss this as merely a "splash party" have no idea what goes on beneath the surface.

Let me fill you in.

For starters, water aerobics is no less a workout than land exercise. We're burning just as many calories as the bouncing bodies looking down at us from the windowed aerobics room above our pool. We're running and jumping, twisting and flexing, just as they are. Both groups are toning muscles, increasing heart rates, and improving balance and posture. But since the thickness of water is greater than air, the increased resistance inherent in water aerobics often results in *more* calories burned and *greater* muscle strength and endurance for us than for our friends exercising upstairs.

The big difference, though, is that we splash. And we do seem to smile more. After all, our buoyancy reduces impact on joints, improves flexibility, and reduces potential for injury.

But that's not the half of it. Let me introduce you to a few of my water aerobics buddies.

Ron comes to class—oxygen tank in tow—every single day. COPD has robbed him of the active retirement he had hoped for, but he's far from sedentary. Even though his lungs aren't working at full capacity, he doesn't stop moving, and his cardiovascular and muscular systems thank him for his efforts. Ron sees it this way: "It gets me out. It keeps me moving."

Sluggish, huh?

With the aid of a cane, Debra hobbles across the parking lot, through a corridor, down the next hallway, and into the locker room, her deformed legs appearing to move in two different directions. She painstakingly changes into her swimsuit—another ten-minute ordeal—then totters out to the pool. Although she's relatively young, Debra has severe hip dysplasia accompanied by chronic, relentless pain. Where years ago she might have been confined to her home, today she fights like a warrior to get to class four to five times a week. "This one hour of aqua exercise can keep me pain-free until seven o'clock tonight," she explains. Hidden beneath the water is a strength that should humble the rest of us.

Languid?

Sarah has spent the past year sleeping most of the day. The reason? Her son committed suicide, thrusting her into a spiral of depression. Paralyzed with grief, fear, even anger, Sarah had neither the strength nor the will to get out of bed each day. A friend nearly dragged her to water aerobics, where she discovered that the endorphins she produces help lift her pain, giving her hope that one day the darkness will retreat for good. Above the surface, we see a listless face, but below, Sarah is driven by the mantra, "Strong arms, strong legs," as she exerts her power over the mass of water that could be oppressive to someone less hardy. In addition to the vigorous exercise, Sarah clearly enjoys the company of people who assure her she's not alone. "This is saving my life," she says. "I have no doubt I'd have a serious illness by now if I were keeping it all inside."

Foo-foo?

Ironically, it's these heroes—who don't *appear* to be in top shape—who give water aerobics the reputation for being a "lazy" sport. Yet no one works harder.

Most of us have the same basic reason for joining the group: to get a workout without overheating or taking a pounding on our joints. There's nothing that stops Ron, Debra, Sarah, or any of us from enjoying a more rigorous workout. Only we are in charge of what happens underwater.

But we're also there for friendship. As anyone who observes a class will notice, water aerobics, in general, is not a silent workout time. It's a chance to meet and interact with vibrant, fascinating people, some still working in colorful careers, some retired. We find support when we're hurting, encouragement when we need it; greeting cards regularly sit on the table poolside to receive our dripping sentiments and signatures of concern after class. And the constant orders from our instructor to "pick it up, pick it up, pick it up!" remind us that as we nurture these friendships, we're also keeping our bodies in shape.

Interesting that when I ask Gerry what Jerry does while she's at her "splash party," she says, "Oh, he's just at home, slugging around."

But Ron, Debra, Sarah, and the rest? Nothing sluggish about us.

Driver's License Angst

A group of teacher friends and I were having dinner. "I have a question for everyone," said Kim, our talented and free-spirited art teacher. "How many of you weigh what it says on your driver's license?"

I choked on my french fry. *Oops. Busted.*

Jill started the volley. "Well, I *was* that weight when I renewed my license five years ago, but I'm probably a good five pounds over right now. I'm going to start a diet next week because I have to renew on my birthday in two months."

Five pounds? That's all?

Sue followed. "It's ten pounds for me."

Then Cheryl. "I'm about fourteen pounds more."

And Val. "I'm up and down, so I don't know what weight to report. So I just tell them what I *wish* I weighed."

Christy offered a different take. "Is it really bad that I said I was forty pounds less? I was eight months pregnant when I renewed my driver's license. I didn't want to report weight that I was going to be losing."

We all rallied around Christy to assure her it was the right thing to do.

Then Kim said it like it was. "Well, I just flat-out lie. I don't weigh anywhere near what it says on my driver's license."

A loud burst of laughter interrupted the calm ambiance of the restaurant. Kim had said what we were all thinking.

But seriously. Given it's such a touchy subject, isn't it a little intrusive for the state to ask us what we weigh? There's a picture of me right on my license, after all. Does my to-the-pound weight shed any more light on my identity?

Let's face it: my own unscientific study has revealed that a lot of us—maybe most of us—fudge the numbers a bit, and give approximations rather than exact figures. If that's good enough for us, then it should be good enough for the state.

If it really matters, then just ask for a weight *range*, and assign each range a letter. For example: under 100 pounds, A; 100–149, B; 150–200, C; over 200, D. And if the state *really* enjoys embarrassing us, they could put little cartoon drawings next to the ranges: A, a face with sunken cheeks; B, a glowing visage with a confident smile; C, a face bearing an expression of shame and disappointment; D, a head covered with a paper bag. This is for women, of course. For men, the scale would have to be shifted up, because we all know the same weight on a man's larger frame looks much different, an inequality even a constitutional amendment can't right.

Ours is a nation obsessed with body image, and when people feel like they need to crash diet every time their driver's licenses come up for renewal, it only causes angst. And for what purpose? It's an outdated form of identification, especially with so much new technology available. Iris recognition, for example, is among the most secure of biometric systems for proving a person's identity.

And that brings up the question of eye color and height on the driver's license. Eye color could depend on whether one is wearing her Ellen-blue contacts that day, so that's a useless piece of information. And as for height, well, as my four-foot-eleven friend Doris explained, she always reports five feet even, because "it's just easier."

So what information is really necessary on a driver's license? Name, address, date of birth, okay. Picture, fine. Organ donor permission, definitely. Blood type? Sure, in case of an accident.

But the weight thing needs to go. Since we're just going to fib anyway to save face in front of anyone who checks our ID, it's neither fair nor necessary to make liars of the whole lot of us.

Pleasure Reading for the Common Good

Call me a visionary, but I've long held the view that there's value in pleasure reading, that literary candy is as important as literary castor oil. Now it's official: an article in the February 3, 2014, edition of *Education Week* reported studies that support that belief. It looks like children who indulge in reading *for pleasure* show "increased cognitive progress over time, which has a significant influence on their educational attainment and social mobility." At the very least, people who read more read better, improve their vocabulary, and gain insight into the human condition.

I've always had a hunch that those who find even a modicum of pleasure in books often become lifelong readers. When I worked as a literacy specialist, I asked a small group of fourth-graders how they chose books.

The answers were fairly predictable for young readers:

"I look at the cover."

"I pick skinny books."

"I make sure there are tons of pictures inside."

Then Dakota spoke. "When I take a book off the shelf, I smell it. If it smells good, I choose that one."

Not three days later, I was telling a group of friends that story.

"Hold on!" Valerie exclaimed. "I need to get something upstairs." She came back cradling a worn tome. "I just bought this at the used book store. Tell me what it smells like to you."

Pat took a sniff. "Oh my gosh—it smells like a 1950s classroom!"

"I know!" said Valerie. "I bought it because it smells like the books I read when I was little."

Ahh, the sensory pleasure of reading.

In education circles, we say the joy of reading belongs to those who have mastered the principles of good literacy instruction. Reading is thinking, we declare. Indeed, we do a good job of teaching comprehension strategies, exposing students to different genres, and developing their analytical skills. But how do we rank in making sure students love to read?

The *experience* of reading, the multisensory quality folded into it—that's where the pleasure lies.

Recall for a moment what made you a book lover.

Slip back in memory to childhood, where you lay in the cool grass reading comic books, a shaft of sunlight cast on the page, overshadowed from time to time by the smooth movement of clouds.

Smell the crisp night air, hear the crackling of the campfire as you laid your head on the lap of the parent or sibling who was reading to you.

Feel the fluffy comforter that swallowed you up in your top bunk, the flashlight you weren't supposed to have barely illuminating the pictures in your bedtime indulgence.

Now let's recreate those experiences for our children.

It seems we have it backward. We start with the premise that we have to bring students up to a certain level of proficiency in reading before they can enjoy it. But for those with dyslexia, second language delays, or other learning challenges, that may not happen. So perhaps if we start by making reading pleasurable—at whatever level the student is reading—we can produce readers who will see literature as their friend, and who, rather than avoiding books, will pounce on the written word for all the right reasons: to appease their curiosity, to become better informed, or simply to relax.

So I propose we add to our Common Core State Standards this common sense standard: "The learner will become a lifelong reader by soaking in the experience itself with all its sensory pleasures."

Never gonna happen, you say? Then let's at least make sure it's a standard in our homes.

Imagine seeing your children in the comfort of their coziest sleepwear, the unrelenting rain or snow consoling them with its invitation to spend the day inside fingering the pages of a delicious book, like young Abe Lincoln holed up in his cabin.

Now that, right there, deserves an A+.

Kidnapped: Caring Enough

I was fifteen years old when a violent murder far away stabbed at my psyche and dumped trauma into my very cells.

"I didn't want to get involved," rang the famous words that over thirty "ear witnesses" in New York had used to exonerate themselves from having let it happen. The chilling screams of a young woman enduring stab wound after stab wound fell on it's-just-a-lovers'-quarrel ears, someone-else-will-help-her ears, I-don't-want-to-get-hurt ears.

The horrific fear that must have engulfed Kitty Genovese settled into my depths and never left.

Through my anger and alarm, my mind developed a mantra that would play over and over in the days and years that followed: "Someone should've, we all could've, but *I* would've."

Would I have?

Cared enough, that is.

In my young heart, I made a promise to myself that if life ever put me in the situation of being a witness, I would act.

Twenty-five years later, it happened.

It was the summer equinox, the longest day of the year, and the sun, sneaking toward the west, begged to extend its bedtime. I was on my way to a prayer group at a church twenty miles from my home near Denver, Colorado, heading north on Wadsworth, a wide, traffic-laden boulevard lined with office buildings, strip malls, and apartments. Car exhaust formed tendrils over warm asphalt, brake lights flashed caution, drivers mindlessly tapped their knuckles on their steering wheels to the music locked inside—a predictable, almost comforting background for my mind as I mentally rehashed my day.

So when a beat-up, older-model vehicle slipped into my lane right in front of me, I barely noticed. Several kids were inside. *Teenagers? Twenty-somethings?* It didn't really matter.

Back to my thoughts.

Suddenly a blur of motion jolted me out of my reverie. *What was that?* My eyes darted to the car ahead. *Hmm. Nothing, I suppose.*

Then it happened again.

Did someone just hit that guy?

Denial instantly engulfed me. *Nah, those are just kids messing around with each other.*

And then it happened a third time.

I'm not wrong. Smacking that boy on the side of the head is exactly what those kids are doing.

Flustered, I wasn't sure what to do. I trailed the car for a while. Then I moved into the next lane and crept up on the hostage-takers. I peered into the window.

A young man sat in the back seat, squished between two thugs who were viciously assaulting him. Tears streamed down his cheeks.

Utter fear.

I glanced frantically at the drivers around me. *Does no one see this?* I desperately wanted someone else to take charge of getting this young man some help.

But no one registered any concern whatsoever.

I don't want to get hurt, I thought. But clearly, it was up to me. Once I accepted that, ideas for rescuing the terrified captive stormed my brain.

Take down the license plate number.

I blindly rummaged through my purse for a pen, then scribbled on the first thing my fingers found: my checkbook.

Note the make and color of the car. I wrote it down.

Stay on his tail. I am, I am!

Be ready in case they turn onto a side street. But if they do, don't be stupid: don't follow them.

Seconds later, my quarry veered off the main road and onto a side street.

Crap. Now what?

Somehow I had the presence of mind to jot down the name of the street and the direction the car was heading.

Still several miles from my destination, and not seeing any open businesses or payphones, I did the only thing I could think of: stepped on the gas and charged down Wadsworth Boulevard—way over the speed limit—hoping a cop would pull me over.

Not a patrol car in sight. *Where are you when I need you?*

I continued to speed, fueled by terror. Finally at my destination, I pulled into the parking lot of the church, bolted for the door, tore into the office and, out of breath and trembling, called the police.

The dispatcher wanted to know my name. "There's no time," I pleaded. "If you don't hurry, they're going to kill that boy."

But in truth, it wasn't about the ten extra seconds it would take to reveal my name. I was struggling with a dilemma I promised I would never find myself in: I didn't want to get involved.

At least any more than I already had.

I didn't want my identity known, didn't want to testify, didn't want to do *everything possible* to save that young man and bring his kidnappers to justice.

I don't want to get involved.

For heaven's sake, Maggie.

Shame filled me.

What happened next was humbling. My own voice called me out—with the same line of admonishment I reserved for my children: "You don't have to *want* to do it. You just have to do it."

So I gave my name to the police.

It had been a long, exhausting day. I retired to the chapel to pray for a call telling me the abductors had been stopped in time. There, my twenty-five-year-old mantra returned, twirling in my head: "Someone should've, we all could've, but I would've."

I had.

At last, the call came. The police had saved my young man.

I had cared enough.

Those Teachers Are At It Again

This vignette was published as a guest commentary in the Denver Post *on May 6, 2014*

Rapping the knuckles of our nation's teachers has gone on long enough. It's time to stop the "they don't work hard enough" putdowns. The disparaging remarks like "those who can't do, teach." Having been a teacher for many years, and having seen those fanatically dedicated folks up close, I tend to be a fan.

Let me set you straight on what they really do.

I'm not going to bore you with stories you've heard a gazillion times about how genuinely caring teachers are. You don't need to hear, yet again, about teachers like my colleague Kathy, who has bought hundreds of books out of her personal income with specific students in mind, based on their unique interests and their reading strengths and weaknesses. Or about Mike, who purchases boots and snow pants for his third-graders every frosty winter because they often come to school without. You don't need me to tell you that teachers put in an awful lot of work during their "free" time. Or that nearly one hundred percent of the educators with whom I've taught are right now raving about their wonderful students, those children they love with every ounce of passion in their hearts. Your child is one of them.

No, no, no. You don't want to hear all that sappy stuff again. You want to hear about the time I pretended it was I who had farted so my student wouldn't be bullied.

So.

It was writing time, and all the kids were engaged in creating their stories. It had taken from August to March to get to this point, where the students could go from outline to final published product almost entirely on their own. In the background, the gentle melodies of my son Timothy Pike's album *All That Matters* provided calm and inspiration. This was—ahem—an exemplary classroom environment.

I invited Sterling—so named because that's what his mother thought he was—to come up to my desk and privately share his writing with me. Sterling not only struggled as a student, but as an emerging teen as well. He was a tall, handsome boy, but he nevertheless exuded a slight vulnerability that certain other sixth-graders seized upon without conscience.

He read his sacred story to me in low tones, stumbling on word after word. I was in awe of his creativity and intrigued by his heartfelt plot. I was also grateful he didn't have to read in front of the class. I did my best to create a bubble of safety during our conference.

Without warning—and in the middle of Sterling's dramatic "And then I was at the sixth level and my brother told me it was his turn and I said no it is my video game I got it for my birthday and then he said . . ."—the silence was shattered by a thunderous *fpfpfpfpfpfpfpfpfpfpfpf*. At least a 7.4 on the rectum scale.

A slight whiff of something followed.

Instantly, every head lifted. Eyes shifted in mirth, lips formed mischievous smirks. All Hades was about to break loose, and Sterling was the target.

Not if I could help it.

Wasting not a second, I looked up, deadpan. "Excuse me. I'm sorry," I announced.

Silence.

With no reaction whatsoever, grins disappeared, heads went down, pencils resumed their race across loose-leaf pages.

Sterling and I continued sharing.

A single moment in time—teachers face hundreds of these in a day. And with each and every split-second decision they make, what's best for your child is uppermost in their minds.

Reporters from the local daily won't be rushing to your school to report each life-giving moment a teacher provides, or every stink torpedo covered for, because it's the occasional slip-up that makes for better press. But I know what teachers are really up to. Believe me, thanks to them, your child has one more reason to grow up knowing he or she is, well, sterling.

So celebrate your teachers. Trust someone who knows: your children are in good hands.

Sweet Justice without Violence

This vignette was published as a guest commentary in the Denver Post *on December 17, 2014*

When something as regrettably monumental as the tragic loss of life in Ferguson, Missouri, when shock and deep mourning grip the nation, and the outcry is day after day of widespread violence, many of us have the same question: what would be a better way?

We all want this to never happen again; change is crucial. But brutality—on either side—can't be our modus operandi as civilized people.

The fact is, every day brings us opportunities big and small to effect justice, and we always have a choice as to how to respond.

A few years ago, I was privy to a scenario that spelled sweet justice without violence. In no way do I compare the gravity of what I saw to the horrendous event in Ferguson. I merely present an outside-the-box way to express rage in a quotidian situation.

It was an overcast day, and Colorado was breaking out in fervent holiday madness. There I was, driving up and down the lot at Park Meadows Mall trying to find a parking place. My mood was already dark, forcing me to gripe about why I had to put up with this when all I needed was a single item from Petsmart. But finally, I found a space way on the outskirts of the mall.

There, I noticed a spanking new Lamborghini parked horizontally in the lot. Picture two adjacent letters—HH—which would normally accommodate four cars, right? Now place the Lamborghini horizontally across the middle H-bars so that it, and only it, can park there.

That Lamborghini took up four parking spaces. *Four.*

I wasn't the only one who saw this as rapacious. But I was about to witness a most extraordinary phenomenon: a scene of communal indignation at its finest.

As I sat in my forlorn gray Honda Civic, a driver pulled up and eyed the arrogant Lamborghini. He paused for a moment, then stationed his black Hyundai Accent into the space right in front of that parking hog.

Remember, the Lamborghini was facing sideways. So now its driver couldn't move forward. The driver got out of his sedan, glared at the Lamborghini, and strode across the parking lot to the Cheesecake Factory.

Right behind the Hyundai, the driver of a tan Toyota was also looking for parking. The brakes went on when she reached the Lamborghini, all regal-like resting on its four-space throne. The driver rolled her eyes, backed up and inserted her car next to the rear of the Lamborghini. Now the guy couldn't back out either.

I was getting giddier by the minute. But the show wasn't over yet.

A blue Kia, its driver desperate for a parking space, slowly dragged the lane. The motorist stopped, took one look at Lamborghini Monster, and threw up her hands. She looked slyly from side to side, then inched her car into the space until her front bumper almost touched the side of the horizontally parked Lamborghini. So now it had the nose of a Kia flush to its driver's door. The Kia driver slipped out of her car and chuckled, then bolted for the Container Store.

The Lamborghini was completely caged in.

Oh. My. Gosh. This was such sweet justice. The human spirit, bonded in righteousness, had pulled off the perfect vindication without a single word exchanged. No harassment, no ugly epithets, no violence.

Just a parade of cars quietly righting a wrong.

Showdown in the Showroom

A few years ago, I dredged up a long-neglected item from my bucket list: I'd always wanted to bargain for a car.

My previous vehicle had come from a "no-haggle" dealership—those big party poopers. But now I was in the market for a car that would last me until the end, one with outstanding gas mileage. Ecologically friendly. A hybrid.

Something previously owned, preferably an even-numbered year. I have a thing for even numbers.

Color? Anything but silver: it doesn't show up very well in rain and snow. Oh, and not beige. I'm not a beige person. Or black—it was so hot that summer that I just couldn't bear the thought of sitting in a black car that was soaking up more heat.

So I went for broke: if I could find a 2010 Toyota Prius in blue, I would consider it a sign.

And by golly, I would fight for it.

To that end, I googled "how to haggle for a car" and found a couple of worthwhile articles. For two days, I brushed up on the finer points of acting tough. I called my sister Mary, a business executive, and asked her how I could look powerful.

"Whenever I'm going to fire someone," Mary explained, "I wear black."

Black. Got it.

"And if I want to make a point with authority, I take my glasses off and give them a firm thrust when I get to the heart of my argument."

"But you don't wear glasses, Mary."

"I know. The dollar store. They're just a prop."

Glasses. Check.

"Oh, or a pen. Equally effective. As long as it's a dignified pen. Nothing that says Bic or First Bank."

I checked to make sure the wood pen my friend Frank had carved for me was easily accessible in my purse. *Got it.*

I awoke the next morning feeling nervous. But after I had donned my black outfit, pulled my hair back, put on my glasses, and peered into the mirror, insight struck.

You're an actress, Maggie. This is your breakout role. Now, shoulders back, head up, lengthen your stride, strengthen your handshake.

And stay in character.

Suddenly, I felt unparalleled confidence.

I grabbed the portfolio I'd prepared of Edmunds car listings with the precomputed 15 percent discount I was going to offer the dealer; Kelly Blue Book rates for my trade-in; individual dealerships' listings (for comparison); preapproved low-interest loan quote from my bank; information about a specific Prius from Avis, which was offering a free three-day test drive (for leverage); a *Time* magazine to casually read when my salesman went back "to check with my boss"; and my dignified pen. The magazine, I'd read online, would give me an air of not caring, of having all the time in the world, which Sales Person and Man Behind the Screen would be assessing as they watched me through surveillance cameras.

I strode into the lobby of the Toyota dealership exactly on time for my appointment with Donny. Through the glass door of his office, I could see Donny nod in acknowledgment of my arrival, then turn back to his computer.

Uh-huh. Keeping me waiting, I see. He's establishing dominance. I read about that in the script.

I sat back in my chair and paged through my magazine. *I'm in no hurry to buy a car.*

Several minutes later, Donny approached me. I was my normal self: kind, sincere, and friendly. No reason to pull out my power card yet. *If I even have one.*

"Well, let's look at some cars, shall we? I have two I think you'll like."

I was suddenly gripped with stage fright. *Can I really do this? Stay in character, Maggie.* I slid into the driver's seat of the first car.

As we drove the newer, fewer-miles Prius 3, I interspersed our small talk with tidbits about my extensive research of hybrids. *Steady voice, go down a pitch, firm tenor.*

I told Donny that time was on my side; I didn't need the car just yet. In fact, I had gone over to Avis to check out the three-day test-drive, and I thought I would probably wait on a decision until I'd tried that one.

"What! You don't want a rental car. Those renters drive 'em into the ground," he said.

"Well, Donny, according to my research, that's one possibility. The other side of the argument is that rental agencies maintain their cars well and sell them at low mileage. So it's not as dramatic as you're making it out to be."

Just sayin'.

"So do you love this car?" Donny probed as we got out. "How's the color for you? Are you pleased with the low mileage?"

"I like the low mileage, but I don't need it to be 6,000 miles. Under 50,000 would work for me. I like the tinted windows, but I don't need all the bells and whistles. What else do you have?"

He took me to his other offering.

A basic Prius 2.

2010.

Blue.

Da-da-DA-da. My sign.

A test drive confirmed that this would be the car I haggled for.

"If we can get the numbers to work, would you be likely to buy this car?"

"Well, let's talk about it, Donny. That's a pretty big *if.* I'm not in a hurry, you know."

Donny introduced me to Snidely, the man who would be evaluating my trade-in. I was offering my daughter's 2001 Mitsubishi, which, admittedly, had seen better days.

"Donny tells me you're thinking of buying a rental from Avis. That's a bad idea." With no eye contact to assure me of even a trace of sincerity, he expounded on the horrors of owning a rental car. I let my eyes wander, too. *Ho-hum. You're just talking 'cause your mouth is moving.*

Exit Snidely.

Donny and I entered the showroom, where tables were scattered across the set at a comfortable distance from each other.

I had learned that car dealers make their money in three ways: 1) their loan to the buyer; 2) the price of the car; and 3) the trade-in.

The negotiation was about to start.

Stay in character. I sat up straight, head held high.

Now, break a leg.

"So, Maggie. Will you be financing through us?" Donny asked casually.

"No, my bank preapproved me at a very low rate. I'll go with them." I mirrored his casualness.

"Hmm. Let me see if we can match that. I'll go ask my boss." *My cue. When he gets up and leaves, either read nonchalantly or get up and leave, too. I headed to the bathroom.*

When I returned to the table, Donny was looking for me.

"Oh, I'm sorry. I had something to do," I said.

Hee hee. This was just plain fun.

"Well, good news. My boss said we can match your bank's interest rate." *Mm-hmm. Am I surprised?*

"Now here's a printout of your costs. The price of the car, taxes and fees, insurance for chipped windows, the value of your trade-in. Just sign here."

"Wait a minute, Donny," I said benignly. "According to Blue Book, $500 for my trade-in is out of the question." *Low-baller.* "I'll tell you what. My daughter works at the University of Denver. She can sell this car to a student. So let's take it off the table completely." *Smooth, Maggie, smooth.*

I thought I heard Donny gulp. "Well, what if I give you $700 for it?"

"For that car? Not even close. As I said, let's just forget the trade. Now tell me about this chipped window insurance. $500? Is that required? Because I don't want it."

"Yeah, it's part of the package. You should see how badly windows get chipped in Colorado."

I've been driving in Colorado since before you were born. But I'm going to let you get away with that manipulative comment.

"And one more thing, Donny. I'm prepared to pay $3,000 less than you're asking."

When you make your offer, stare him in the eyes. Most people start to stammer and apologize after making an offer.

I stared him in the eyes.

This time he did gulp.

"Well, I don't have any control over that," he countered.

"Who does?"

"The man you met earlier about your trade-in."

"Snidely? Well, please ask Snidely if he's willing to sell me this car for $3,000 less." *Sustain eye contact.*

"Maggie, $3,000 is a huge amount. My boss isn't going to go for it. Will you meet me halfway? $1,500 off?"

If they won't take 15 percent, which they probably won't, take the compromise. And always give a reason why you're offering less. Amenities, too. Ask for some amenities.

"You know, Donny, this car isn't proportionately priced to the Prius 3 we drove. It has five times the mileage, plus it doesn't have a back-up mirror or GPS like that one did, and it doesn't have tinted windows. I really wanted tinted windows."

"I can give you tinted—"

"Okay, I'll take the tinted windows and $1,500 off the price of the car. And it's a no-go on the trade-in."

Star quality, girl.

Donny disappeared. I headed to the drinking fountain.

When I returned, I located the camera, turned my chair toward it, pulled up another chair, put my feet up, and read my *Time* magazine.

Stay in character. Your audience is watching you.

Donny returned with a new printout.

"Good news, Maggie. Here's what we're going to do. $500 off the price of the car, 50 percent off the chipped window insurance, only $100 for the tinted windows and we'll pay the rest, and $1,000 for your trade-in. Sign here and it's yours."

I straightened my ebony collar and adjusted my glasses.

"Let's see here," I said, perusing the printed counteroffer. "No, I know we can get a lot more for the trade-in by selling privately. Some student at DU would love to have a commuter like that one."

"Well, selling it at the university's going to be a hassle," he assured me.

"Well, no it's not," I assured him right back. "So again, let's take that off."

I continued reading his offer, running my dignified, hand-carved pen down the list.

"Oh, gosh. Half off the price of chipped window insurance. That's nice of you, but really, Donny, I don't want insurance. I sure wish it weren't part of the price of the car, even at 50 percent off. And how is it I'm paying $100 for free tinted windows?"

Donny huffed. "Okay, I'll take that off. If tinted windows are that important to you . . ."

"They are. Thank you."

Man, you can't pay for entertainment like this.

I pointed at the price of the car.

"Donny, what happened to the $1,500 we agreed on? This still says $500 off."

He sulked again. "Okay, will you meet me halfway? $750 off?"

"No. I already met you halfway once and you didn't live up to your part of the bargain."

"I'll tell you what I'll do. I'll scratch the window insurance."

Suddenly, a tempest brewed within me.

I ripped my glasses from my face and shook both them and the dignified, wooden pen at Donny. "That's not a discount. Taking off insurance that I never wanted in the first place is not giving me a break in price. It's taking away a service." Now I was out of character. Or I was a new character, a shrew. I wasn't sure which.

But he was messing with me, and that's when I get mad.

Get a grip, Maggie. You're a professional.

I softened my voice.

"Donny, look." I put my glasses back on. "I think you're a good person."

"Oh, I am. I'm a really good person. Honest I am."

"I know," I said. "But I don't like it when you play tricks on me. Ignoring our compromise, charging me for free tinted windows, and telling me you're giving me a deal by removing an unwanted service from your offer makes me think you think I'm stupid. Not appreciated, my friend."

Donny looked down and put his hands on his head. "This is such a hard job. I want to make you happy and I want you to have the car you want, but then I have to listen to my boss yell at me every time I go back and tell him what you want."

"I understand, Donny." I almost felt sorry for him. Almost. "Now, if you'll go back and ask Snidely for $1,000 more off this car, you've got a sale."

I have never been this gutsy in my life. Where is this coming from?
Donny hesitated.

"You know, Maggie, I do have one other car I could show you that might be closer to your price range."

I nodded. "Yes, let's look at that one," I said. "I'm thinking I'd rather get something less expensive. Either that or I'll just take a couple of weeks to think about all this. I don't really have to have a new car right now." *You little bluff-caller, you.*

"I should tell you it's, uh . . ." He cleared his throat and avoided my eyes. "It's a rental."

No.

Tell me he didn't just say that.

I slid my glasses to the end of my nose and stared over them right into his eyes. I didn't say a word. I didn't need to.

Donny finally broke the silence. "But let's see if we can get you into this Prius because I know you really like it."

Again he disappeared, and again I whipped out my magazine. Blasée. Laid back. Detached. I'd never read *Time* from cover to cover, but I did that day.

Donny returned with his closing offer.

Final scene of the showdown. The curtain was ready to fall.

Donny still gave me only $500 off the price of the car, so he got his healthy commission.

But he now offered $1,500 on my trade-in, free tinted windows, no chipped-glass insurance, plus $250 off for no particular reason, so I won, too.

That was the best part of the adventure—we both won.

But I was spent. Getting my part of the win, that was about all the toughness I had in me.

Fifth Glass
BLUSH

Blush

My neighbor JoAnn stood in my kitchen groping for the glass door that was already open. Finally realizing her mistake, she blushed. "Gee, what am I doing? I'm so embarrassed."

"Embarrassed for what?" I wondered.

"Oh, for being human," she said as she stalked away, her head down.

That's just it. We're all so very human.

And we take such pains to hide it.

Human is Ann trying to impress her colleagues as a trail of toilet paper streams behind her. Human is Jeff sporting the bloodied and crumpled tissue on his chin from his shaving cut as he waves to the neighbors, drives to the airport, parks in the lot, takes the crowded shuttle to the terminal, checks his bags, rides the jam-packed train to his gate, climbs over his row-mates and plops down in his seat before he scratches his chin and makes the horrible discovery. Human is Nora at the gym, sliding on her bare rear end across the shower room floor, stopped only by a row of metal lockers.

I've met people who truly can't remember a single embarrassing moment. I envy their certitude about themselves. Others harbor embarrassment as if its release will destroy them. But I find the best way to free the grip of embarrassment is to simply admit it and let the blushing begin. I myself buried my most embarrassing incident for years until, in a moment of intoxicated candor, I suppose, I threw all caution to the wind and just told it. It was cathartic.

Like a blush wine, delicate in color and flavor, pairing easily with almost any meal, blushing persons are appealing, mixing easily with just about anyone. We can relax in their presence because we know they're real. So imbibe these stories and feel the warm rising of color to your cheeks. And if nothing else, be grateful you're not one of these people.

They're way too human.

But since I'm proud to be part of the human race, I'll go ahead and start the blushing—er, sharing.

Trapped at Water World

It was a suffocating day in July and as far as I was concerned, there was only one solution.

"Come on, kids, get your swimsuits! We're heading to Water World."

The whooping erupted and didn't cease until we rolled into the enormous, steaming parking lot at Eighty-Eighth and Pecos Streets, just north of Denver, Colorado. Within seconds, the car was empty and all of us had scattered to our favorite areas of the park.

Let it be said that I can—and did—tear down the Ragin' Colorado, Screamin' Mimi, and Tandemonium with the best of them, but as the day wore on, Tortuga Run was calling to me. That Tortuga, an island in the West Indies off northern Haiti, was a pirate refuge in the seventeenth century, didn't even occur to me. I just knew it was the Spanish word for turtle, and by four o'clock in the afternoon, I was ready to slow down.

To give you a picture, Tortuga Run is an easygoing jaunt down a series of alternating chutes and whirlpools. The first chute gently deposits the tube rider into an eddy, which swirls that person around a few times, then leads him or her down another chute and into the next whirlpool, and so forth.

Benign. Chill. Tortuga-like.

When my turn came, I plopped down onto the inner tube, rear end in the opening, feet straight out in front of me. Down I went.

Whoosh! Sheer delight.

Now the whirlpool. *Ahhhh, fun.*

Then the next chute. *Weeeeeee!*

Into the second eddy I slid.

Gee, I seem to be going awfully fast. Right in front of me was a man who hadn't left the pool yet and was still drifting around and around. *Come on, Buster, move! Get over, I'm on my wayyyyyyyy—*

Splash! Thud. Abrupt halt.

Oh. My. Goodness.

My eyes were staring right into the face of Buster.

And my foot . . .

My foot was stuck, how shall I say this . . . jammed in? Locked? Okay, *right between* this man's legs. Tight.

Do I need to spell this out for anyone?

We were trapped, to say the least.

Anyone watching us would have seen two unruffled adults lazing in the pools of Water World as if we were old friends enjoying a drink together. In reality, my new gentleman friend and I were equally aghast, which I knew because we both immediately shifted our eyes to stare nonchalantly at the blue sky above. *Huh. Love those clouds. We can use the shade.*

Tragically, I couldn't move my foot too much because, well, you know. Feeling frantic, I craned my neck to see if the guard with the long bamboo pole would notice our predicament without my having to shout for help in front of God-and-everyone. But he was looking elsewhere.

Meanwhile, with the two tubes now swirling together as one, the current was too weak to push us to the mouth of the chute. So around and around we went, both of us digging our hands into the water to fight the vortex, all the while maintaining our casual demeanor, feigning interest in the bird over there, the tree over here. Each of us desperately struggled to escape, yet neither one dared look at the other in the process.

I broke into a sweat. *This is never going to end.*

After what seemed like four, possibly five, long hours, I saw the lifeguard's welcome pole approach us. I grabbed that thing and tugged as hard as I could, fighting the current and my partner's—shall we say, grip—with all the adrenaline that filled me, until finally, and at long last . . . *ahh!* My emancipated foot and I sailed together down the chute to sweet freedom.

I never looked back.

Mountain Biking Debacle

Sky, so named for her initials rather than for any resemblance to Sky King from 1950s television, nevertheless shared the same penchant for adventure as the fictional Arizona aviator. But instead of a Cessna 310 airplane named Songbird, this Sky had her mountain bike to bring her soaring from out of the clear blue of the western sky.

And that's exactly how she had spent her Saturday. Although Sky's goal was to one day own a Cannondale Scalpel 29er Carbon Ultimate mountain bike, a mere $11,000 purchase, she had stretched her high school counselor budget as far as she could and was right proud of the bike she did own. She clamped her treasure securely onto the roof of her 1990 Honda and set off down Interstate 70 to her home in suburban Denver.

It had been a spectacular day in the Colorado Rockies. As she drove, Sky rolled her shoulders and stretched her calves, their stiffness reminders of her remarkable feat. With the help of a nice tailwind, she'd broken her speed record, reaching forty-five miles per hour. At one point, her steering control became a little iffy and she began to spin, but regaining control was no problem. She considered herself a pro, not by biking standards perhaps, but she knew what she was doing. Next time she was going to break fifty miles an hour, a modest goal, really, compared to some who claimed they had reached upward of seventy-five.

Those were the thoughts that absorbed Sky as she turned into her driveway, pressed the garage door opener, and drove into her parking space.

Bang!

Clang!

Crunch.

What the . . . ? Sky got out of her car to find the source of the noise.

There was her mountain bike.

Bent in half.

The top of the garage door smirking at her.

Fortunately, the bicycle repair shop was open the next day, and the proprietor greeted Sky as he would a good biking buddy who shared his passion and prowess.

"Whoa, well, will you look at that?" he said. "What happened here?" Sky wasn't sure, but thought she picked up a tone of admiration in the man's voice. *Might as well play along,* she decided.

"Yeah, I hit a big one," she lied. "Thirty-five . . . uh, forty miles an hour down Vail Pass, rounded the corner, and there she was. No time to stop."

"Well, that's one for the books," the man said. "Come on in. Let's see what we can do."

This was not a cheap snafu, as Sky learned the next Friday when she picked up her mountain bike. *But I guess I learned a lesson,* she assured herself as she clamped her newly repaired gem securely onto the roof of her Honda and set off for home. Her mind drifted to her weekend plans. More mountain biking, of course. She was stoked about trying out Winter Park this time. Her neighbors were letting her use their cabin, and she'd invited a couple of friends to go along. Skies were predicted to be vintage Colorado clear, the famed 350-days-a-year sun befriending her as she would whizz past the miles of pine trees that lined the switchback-laden mountain pass.

Those were the thoughts that absorbed Sky as she turned into her driveway, pressed the garage door opener, and drove into her parking space.

Bang!

Clang!

Crunch.

Dang.

This time Sky simply backed out and headed in the other direction. To a different bike shop.

Blunder

Even as an adult, Myles cringes when he thinks about the time he inadvertently incited an adjective revolt in his classroom by committing a blunder of epic proportions.

Sixth grade. Language Arts. Lesson: adjectives.

"Let's try to be creative," his teacher began. "Let's not stick with boring, common descriptors."

Myles liked his teacher well enough, but she was so loud and her voice so nasal, she sounded to him like a horn with a plunger mute.

Hee hee. Plunger. He laughed to himself at his quasi-bathroom joke.

Sometimes, in private, he'd attempt to imitate her voice, because it seemed almost impossible for anyone to sound that much like—he could never quite put his finger on it—a trombone? A French horn?

"Are you ready, students?" the teacher blared. "I'll give you an adjective and you combine it with a noun."

Myles welcomed the activity. Words were kind of a hobby for him. He thought it was fun choosing the perfect word to describe a noun.

"Let's start. Red!"

"The red fire engine!" shouted impulsive Peter.

"A red checker!" proposed another.

As his classmates continued casting clichés across the room, Myles was busy mentally concocting unique adjective-noun combinations. He was going to revolutionize this lame brainstorming session. If he was anything, after all, he was creative.

Myles mused. *Red—the blood of angry men!* He might've heard that in a song or something, but it was sure better than a boring fire truck. *Blood-red anger,* he decided at last. But he kept it to himself.

"Black!" his teacher bellowed, sounding more like a car horn this time.

"The black police car?" Carrie suggested cautiously.

Black—the dark of ages past! Or better yet, *the black past of a dark age.* Or a bl—

"Red!"

The teacher's shrill voice interrupted Myles's mental attempt to polish his adjective image.

"How about red licorice? And the red sunset." Priscilla always gave two answers. Always.

Red—a world about to dawn! was what popped into Myles's mind. That might've been from a song, too. But again, he kept mum. He didn't want to intimidate his less innovative comrades who didn't know about this talent he harbored.

"Black!"

"I got one! I got one!" It was eager-to-please Scott. "My cat is black."

Oh brother. More like black—the night that ends at last! A black night, ebony night, dreary dimness. Myles's mother was a high school English teacher in the same school; he heard words like this at home sometimes.

His creative juices wouldn't stop flowing, and Myles wasn't sure he could contain his genius much longer.

"Excellent examples, boys and girls," the teacher screeched. Myles silently disagreed, but he did appreciate her alliteration.

Then things took an awkward turn. "Let's go around the room and everyone give one sentence that describes me," the teacher said, her smile shooting beams up and down the rows.

The adjectives flew about like hyperactive ping-pong balls.

"My teacher is tall."

"My teacher is pretty."

My teacher this, my teacher that, my teacher my teacher my teacher . . .

All the answers blended together as Myles sat at the back of row four awaiting his turn. He wanted to create a new adjective, one that described something exceptional about his teacher. He thought again about her voice: The low, smoky sound. Loud, at times, like a staccato trumpet blast; other times lethargic, like the lazy growl of a foghorn. An idea was evolving, an adjective to beat all adjectives.

The litany continued, mere background noise as his turn approached:

"My teacher is smart."

Hurry up . . .

"My teacher is funny."

"My teacher is kind."

Finally it was Myles's turn, and he could contain himself no longer.

"Horny! My teacher is horny!" Myles blurted out, then sat back in his seat, grinning, waiting for the shower of compliments.

Utter silence.

His teacher's face grew red and, speechless, she walked out of the room, where she remained for several minutes. Frantic whispers darted across the classroom.

Myles didn't get it.

When she returned, she asked, "Myles, do you know what that adjective means?"

Myles was confused. "It means you have a voice that sounds like . . . a horn."

The snickering behind him told Myles that might not be what it meant.

"Why?"

"Myles. Either I can tell you what it means, or you can go down the hall and ask your mother."

He chose his mother. And then he blushed.

From that day forward, Myles relinquished his goal of reforming the quality of adjectives in his sixth-grade classroom. After ribbing that wouldn't quit from his buddies and his brothers, and after enduring knowing looks from faculty members, Myles tucked his creative vocabulary into the recesses of his brain and played it safe. From that day forward, the sun was hot, the night was dark, and his teacher was nice.

Crappy Diem

Mary Ann had decided to challenge herself to work past her Latin teacher's thick Russian accent and learn all the conjugations and how to use them—the way the ancient Romans intended.

"I veel explain vy Lateen ees dead," the instructor expounded one day. "Just before Rome croombled in tree 'oondred Anno Domini, Lateen croombled too. Der vas alvays classical Lateen and Vulgar Lateen. Classical vas de langvage of de elite. De common citizen spoke Vulgar Lateen. So did de conquered lands."

Suddenly Mary Ann was distracted by a warmth on her inner thighs, and knew right away what it was.

It's been thirty days already? Oh, boy. What am I gonna do?

She mentally calculated how long it would take to dash from her desk and out the door. *But I can't leave in the middle of class,* she thought. *Everyone'll see. This is a bona fide flood.*

The teacher, meanwhile, droned on ad nauseum: "Ven classical Lateen died, de Vulgar Lateen remained. It vas called Romance langvage. De countries born out of de Roman Empire spoke Romance langvages: Spain, France, Italy, Romania, Portugal."

Mary Ann was beside herself as the flow increased. *Carpe diem,* she swore under her breath. *More like crappy diem.* That was the kind of day it was turning into. She could feel her tartan skirt turning wetter with every minute that passed. All she could do, though, was maintain the status quo until the bell rang at 10:10.

By now, Mary Ann had given up on taking notes, and just hoped the information wouldn't be on the test. Finally, her teacher closed his lecture with the emphatic words: "But *vee,* my students, *vee* vill learn classical Lateen. It ees dead, but *vee* are alive."

The bell rang.

Mary Ann slouched in her seat until everyone had left. The trick would be to slip out before the classroom filled again with the next group of students. She squeezed her legs together and hobbled out the door to freedom. Once in the bathroom—ipso facto terra firma to her—she finally stopped the flow.

But it wasn't over yet.

The next morning, minutes before Latin class was over, the teacher made an announcement.

"Yisterday, somevun left a large amount of blood on der seat. It vas somevun from dees class. Vee vill not leave until dees somevun admits to vot dey did. It vas vulgar, students."

Mary Ann was horrified. As if yesterday were not embarrassing enough, this was ten times worse. Her prayer that a deus ex machina would swoop down and save her went unanswered. How could she admit what she'd done?

Minutes dragged on, and finally Mary Ann did what she had to do. She jumped out of her seat and shouted, "Mea culpa! You're right. I cut my finger on the desk and I should have cleaned it up."

With no indictment whatsoever, her classmates filed out of the room, leaving Mary Ann to wipe the beads of sweat off her brow.

Altar of the Lord

The church was packed to the rafters, and a patchwork of colorful attire splayed across the pews. The simple altar, draped in a pristine, white cloth, set off two elaborate floral displays that jutted upward on either side, left over from a wedding the day before. Small, red candles flickered off to one side, winking an invitation to come before God in supplication. The setting was as serene as a celestial fresco.

This was a special day for Karen and Chuck. As part of the baptism preparation team for the parish, they were ready to lead a procession of parents, godparents, and six infants to the front of the church for the ceremony. Karen and Chuck knew these parents well. They had all spent weeks preparing for this—the first step of imparting their faith to their newborns. Karen herself was just three months from welcoming her own child, so she felt especially close to these parents.

Clearly, the congregation was excited, too. Who doesn't love babies? As soon as Chuck, Karen, and the guests of honor approached the altar, all eyes shifted to them. It was tradition for fellow parishioners to stand as witnesses at baptisms, a sign that they supported the parents in their vocation as primary religious educators of their children. Karen and Chuck had witnessed many baptisms themselves. But this—being such an intimate part of these families' lives, and seeing hundreds of people in attendance at this sacramental ceremony—was bliss.

All these lofty thoughts were floating through Karen's mind as she approached the altar. Donned in a new maternity dress and high heels, she was happy to cast off her sweats and tennis shoes and dress up for a day.

She stopped at the end of the aisle and paused next to Chuck until the others caught up. Then she stepped up into the sanctuary, unable to see her feet below her protruding belly. Without warning, Karen felt herself flying forward, unable to stop herself.

Oops.

Karen was mortified. She quickly straightened her skirt to minimize exposure. Then she slowly pulled herself up, turned to the priest and the parents nearby, and uttered out of the side of her mouth: "I throw myself onto the altar of the Lord."

After private twitters around the sanctuary, the baptism commenced.

Seeking a Bit o' Fiber

School was out for the summer at the university in Alcala de Henares, Spain, and that meant just one thing for Giana and her two friends, Pia and Elisa: travel. They would traverse all of Europe and return home the cultured, world-wise college women they knew they had become.

All three were striking beauties. Elisa was a tall, blond bombshell. Pia, of Indian blood, bore her attractiveness in her bronze skin and luminescent, black hair. Petite, vivacious Giana exuded her zest for life through a California-healthy glow and a hunger for adventure.

You couldn't miss this threesome.

Except the time Giana did miss the other two after they boarded a train to Budapest without her. Fortunately, Giana was able to relay a message to them by describing to the conductor what they looked like ("Yes, tall, blond. Very beautiful. Short, dark. Very beautiful. What's that? Oh, you did notice them? Please ask them to wait for me at the train station when they get off. I'll be there one hour later.")

Yes, these three were standouts, but sometimes Giana wished they weren't. Such was the case the day she woke up with stomach discomfort.

After an entire year studying in Spain, the girls had been ready to cut loose a bit. Country by country, they'd made their way across Europe, eating and drinking their way to Berlin. Tapas and Cruzcampo beer in Madrid, hors d'oeuvres and aperitifs in Paris, Hungarian stuffed peppers washed down with gassy lagers in Budapest, schnitzel and sauerkraut and stouts at various villages in Germany.

But now, this international smorgasbord of rich delights was not quite sitting right with Giana. She needed to find some relief.

In Berlin for the Techno Love Parade, Giana and her friends didn't want to miss a beat of the biggest festival of electronic music in the world, where hordes of locals and visitors would fill the major shopping boulevard, the Kurfurstendamm. As they prepared to leave their hostel, Giana begged Pia and Elisa to stop at the nearby health food store so she could find something to treat her ailing gut.

As soon as the three entered the shop, they unwittingly found themselves caught up in a cultural phenomenon: the volley of the *bittes*. Her language studies had included little to no German, but Giana did know that the word *bitte* went far in Germany; it took on many meanings depending on context.

"Bitte!" said the saleswoman. She was inviting Giana to come in.

"Ja, bitte?" the clerk added. *What can I do for you?*

"Bitte," Giana said, already knowing she was in over her head. She wanted her *bitte* to mean "please."

"Bitte?" *Well?*

"Bitte," replied Giana. *I'm sorry.*

She didn't know how to move forward with the conversation.

Maybe this woman speaks English. "Do you have any fiber?" Giana ventured.

The clerk looked confused. "Bitte?" *I beg your pardon?*

Maybe she knows Spanish. "Fibra?"

The woman's eyes lit up. "Ach! Fever!" She led Giana to the fever-reducing remedies. "Na bitte!" *There you are.* She beamed, happy to have solved the problem.

For Giana, this was proving impossible. *If "fiber" and "fibra" don't trigger anything for this person, what more can I do?* Giana refused to simply shout the word, as so many foreigners do, to no avail, when they aren't understood.

She had no choice but to resort to pantomime.

By now, it seemed the entire neighborhood had gathered in the health food store. So she turned her back to the crowd and spoke under her breath to the saleswoman. "I . . . can't . . . I . . . can't . . . uh . . ." Giana gripped her stomach, then swept her hands downward toward the floor. "Bitte? Bitte?" *Please understand, please. Pretty please?* She distorted her face into a grimace and brushed her hands from stomach to floor again, and again, and again, until the clerk understood at last.

"Ach! Faser. Bitte! Ja!" The code had been broken at last. *Faser.* Elisa and Pia tried their best to shield Giana from her indignity by encircling her like bodyguards, but it appeared she was nonetheless the target of gestures and giggles from many of the German patrons who had come in.

Giana paid for her purchase. "Danke," she said, keeping her eyes down. This woman knew way too much about her.

"Bitte." *My pleasure.*

Giana, Elisa, and Pia darted out the door, Giana gulping the bitter potion as if it were iced tea. Then they headed for the techno parade where, once relief engulfed her, she would at last forget her woes and simply enjoy Berlin.

But the warning label on the bottle—all in German, of which she could read not a word—had completely eluded her: "Drink with plenty of water to avoid expansion of fiber and subsequent severe pain."

"Oh, bitte," Giana muttered that night in the company of the cutest boys in all of Germany. This time, it meant, "You've got to be kidding me."

The Secret Life of Jeans

Jane had always lived a fairly quiet, easygoing life until—well, until the day she caused all hell to break loose.

She swears she didn't mean to.

September of 1990-something was an exciting yet disquieting time for Jane. She was starting college. Some college, somewhere. The details are vague because of the ghastly nature of her embarrassing event. The preparations began in August with trips to Target for bedding, wall hangings, linens, and trinkets for her tiny but charming dorm room.

And jeans. She had to have cool jeans for college. For these, she would go to the mall.

The bustling, two-tiered shopping center was electric with the enthusiasm of back-to-school shoppers. Jane trekked from store to shop to boutique, intent on finding the perfect pair of jeans. They had to be comfortable, of course, but not at the expense of not being "in." No, college was too important to be walking around in uncool clothes.

The following week, Jane hugged her new jeans before placing them in her suitcase. A shivery excitement swept through her as she headed off to her new life. Would she be able to find her way around? Would her classes be too hard? Would she make friends, maybe even meet Mr. Right? Would she and her roommate hit it off? Would her jeans be cool enough? The unknown was unsettling, but oh so alluring.

A week into the school year, something was troubling Jane. Her roommate had jeans that were not only faded, but had holes in them as well. So did a lot of other students on campus. In fact, Jane was starting to feel a little dorky sporting her spanking new jeans.

That night, she took the risk of sounding naive. "Hey, where'd you find those jeans?" she asked her roommate, whose name will also remain unspecified. Horrific story, remember.

"Oh, easy. I had jeans like yours, but then I bleached 'em."

I can do that, thought Jane. *Tomorrow, I'll be cool.*

The next morning after her roommate had left for class, Jane got to work. She couldn't locate the bleach right away, so she grabbed a bottle of ammonia—*same thing, right?*—filled the bathtub, and submerged the denim. With that, she turned her attention to her homework, and awaited the transformation.

An hour passed. No change—the ammonia didn't appear to be working. *What could be wrong? And where is that bleach?* She looked around her roommate's side of the room and finally found it under her desk, of all places. *Great, this'll speed things up.* She added the bleach to the ammonia-filled tub, and the reaction was instantaneous. No, not the fading. The *reaction.* The *chemical* reaction.

The bathroom immediately filled with a thick fog as dense vapors erupted from the tub and permeated the air. Noxious fumes attacked Jane with a vengeance, scorching her lungs. She coughed and choked, feeling weaker by the second. Then she looked up and noticed the fumes were creeping toward the doorway that led to the main corridor.

Frantic, Jane called the resident assistant. "It's not a fire!" she screamed into the phone. "But my room is full of gas or something, and I can't breathe."

The R.A. didn't waste a second pulling the fire alarm. But he practically had to drag Jane out of her room, stricken as she was with a combination of shock, denial, and embarrassment. The hallways were clogged with students calmly filing out, and as she joined them, Jane heard the wailing sirens of approaching fire trucks. Adding a brutal punch to her mortification, the blaring alarm could be heard all over campus.

The entire dormitory gathered outside to escape the poison, but no one breathed in the fresh air more deeply than Jane. Then she slinked to the back of the crowd, speaking to no one, vowing to keep her secret forever.

But when a dozen burly firefighters in full gear marched resolutely into the building, questions began darting through the mystified crowd:

"Why were we evacuated?"

"Bomb?"

"Fire?"

"Who did this?"

Minutes later, the fire crew burst out through the front doors and strode past the crowd like a ticker tape parade. The audience broke into applause, then drew in a collective gasp when their heroes held up the captured villain: Jane's jeans, by now a soggy blob of discolored denim, with fresh, toxic steam still rising from the gaping, newly burned holes.

Jane looked down in silent shame, then gradually realized her saving grace: she was still wearing her sweatpants. Embarrassment turned to relief, Jane happy that, for once, she wouldn't attract attention with her coolness.

Redeemed

The restaurant dripped with prestige, and Jen was ready to play the part. Fresh out of law school, she had just arrived at one of the fanciest restaurants in town for a networking meeting with her mentor, Laura.

It wasn't Jen's idea to meet at a restaurant. She'd spilled enough sauces and condiments on her clothing to know better than to put herself in a potentially embarrassing situation. But there she was anyway, determined to concentrate on each lift of the fork, every sip of her beverage, any morsel that could possibly escape her lips and end up where it shouldn't. She had practiced all week in the privacy of her apartment, and after going three days in a row without tipping over a single cup or sloshing even one drop of soup onto her practice duds, she felt ready.

As Jen waited in the ornate lobby for Laura to arrive, she smoothed her power suit one more time and lifted her eyeglasses from her clutch purse. Jen didn't actually wear glasses, but she was savvy about image, and knew that dark frames, when perched just right on the nose, projected dignity, professionalism, and all things lawyerly. Moreover, punctuating sentences with a thrust of one's glasses suggested knowledge and expertise. She needed that today.

With a deep breath, Jen prepared to impress her mentor.

"Jen, I'm so glad you found the place." Startled by the voice behind her, Jen whipped around. *Oh boy,* she thought. Laura looked every bit the commanding attorney she was.

"Oh, of course." Jen thought about adding that she had been there before many times, but instead resorted to the truth. "Thank goodness for GPS."

The two women followed the maître d' to their table. The menu, printed with large, flowery letters, held a plethora of options, but Jen already knew she was going to order something that went with white wine. Red was too risky, although she'd deliberately worn a dark suit for the very purpose of camouflaging any spills.

The waiter appeared, and Jen cleared her throat. "I'll try the striped sea bass with a glass of Oaky Chardonnay," she said, throwing in a French guttural "r" for effect. Knowing that Oaky had received a bad rap among wine aficionados—she had learned that while researching the pairing of white wines and seafood on the internet—she felt compelled to disclose her reasoning: "I like to match a full-bodied wine with a full-bodied dish."

"That sounds good," said Laura. "I'll have the same."

Jen was pleased—and a little surprised—that her mentor had followed her lead.

As the two made small talk, the bread basket arrived. But when Jen reached for her butter knife, she noticed something she hadn't prepared for: lining each side of her plate was a row of utensils, some of which she'd never even seen before. *Oh no, what am I gonna do?* She ran her finger under her collar, hoping more air would abate the heat that was creeping up her neck. Fortunately, the problem-solving skills she'd sharpened as a law student quickly produced a solution: *I'll just do whatever Laura does.*

The strategy worked, and feeling more comfortable, Jen delved into deeper topics with her mentor, keeping her timbre low and firm as a confident lawyer should. Soon, talk of plaintiffs, pleas, and peremptory challenges was flying across the table, and Jen felt more and more optimistic about her chances for a position with a prominent law firm in the near future.

Suddenly, something small and shadowy appeared in her peripheral vision. *What's that? A fly?* She waved her hand to shoo it away, but it remained. As Laura continued to speak animatedly, probably saying something important, Jen could barely concentrate. *Did my glasses crack? Is the tag still on?*

Then she saw the culprit. Butter meant for her roll had somehow found its way onto her right lens. *How typical,* she admonished herself. Jen's mind was going in a million different directions as she tried to formulate a rejoinder to her mentor's musings—and attempt to redeem herself at the same time.

In an instant of clarity, Jen did what any quick-thinking attorney-to-be would do. With a flick of her hand, she pulled the glasses off her face, thrust them with authority toward Laura, and emphatically stated her case as the butter flew off the glasses and onto her napkin, which she casually laid back on her lap.

Busted

"Yeah, babe. We'll work it out. Uh-huh. Yeah. Sure. Sure. Sure. Okay, she's ready for me. Gotta go. Love you."

Jeff whisked his phone from sight just as his therapist swung open the door. He and Jill had been seeing Marigold as a couple for the last six months, but today she'd invited Jeff to come by himself. *Good thing,* thought Jeff. *I can say what I really think.*

After seven years of marriage and two small children, he and Jill had encountered a rough patch. He loved her and everything, but over the years he'd been conditioned to simply bite his tongue and keep the peace. His passiveness showed during their counseling sessions, too—he didn't dare tell his side of the story because he knew he'd pay for it later. But that day he took on new resolve. He would just tell it like it was. What did he have to lose?

The forty-five minutes flew by as Jeff poured out his frustrations about Jill in the safety of Marigold's office. He had loved her at first, but just two years into the marriage, he started to see her flaws. The decisiveness he once admired in her now felt like bossiness. Her independence had morphed into selfishness. Her people skills, which at first had balanced well with his quiet nature, now seemed to take her away from him all the time. She spent money without consulting him. Building her career was more important to her than he was. While she claimed that childbearing and stress had caused her to gain weight, he was sure she was doing it intentionally just to make herself unattractive to him. He didn't like the chaotic way she got the kids ready and out the door for daycare every morning, and come to think of it, bedtime was just as frenzied. She constantly nagged at him to pitch in, but he honestly didn't know how to help.

The more Jeff talked, the more he convinced himself that he'd made a big mistake marrying Jill. Now that he thought about it, he wasn't even sure he wanted to fight for his marriage. But he did feel better after giving his therapist a more accurate view of the state of their relationship than she had previously heard.

Jeff walked out of the room with a lighter weight on his shoulders. Within seconds, Marigold's phone rang.

"What the f@!%?" barked an instantly familiar voice on the other end of the line. "How can you believe that bas@#!%? And when you agreed with him about the . . . And telling him to tell me . . . And . . ."

Flames almost literally flew out of Marigold's phone. As the tirade continued on the other end, she set the phone down on the table and walked out to the waiting room, where Jeff was still putting on his coat.

"Uh, Jeff?" she said. "I think your wife is trying to get ahold of you. You might want to hang up your phone so she can get through. Apparently she heard our whole session."

He was busted. In the end, Jeff and Jill didn't return for further counseling.

Good Chemistry

There, done.

Gus yawned as he zipped his suitcase shut. *Now I just have to do four interviews in one day,* he thought. It wasn't going to be easy, but he had spent weeks researching each company, and he felt ready. Packing his bag was the last item on his list of preparations. Now it was three a.m. and time to head for the airport.

Security lines were long, as always, so Gus spent the extra time going over the facts about each firm in his mind. All four interviews sounded promising, but he was curious to see what would stand out at each meeting. Even though he was qualified for all the jobs, he knew from previous experience that even the smallest hunch—or misgiving—about a job, organization, or potential boss could make or break an opportunity.

And he also knew that every bit as important as his knowledge was the chemistry between employer and candidate. His expertise was rock solid. But would they like him? Would he appear confident, engaged, and curious? Would they appreciate his brand of friendliness? Would there in fact be chemistry?

And did he smell okay?

Oh no. Gus started to panic. *Did I bring my deodorant?* He'd been in such a rush to pack. *Yes, I think so. But what about the mouthwash?* His confidence was wavering as he approached the TSA agent.

It must have shown.

"Sir, over there please." The latex-gloved agent motioned Gus to a table, where all his toiletries had been laid out, including his deodorant. *Whew.* "Sir, you're supposed to keep these in a *Ziploc* bag and take the entire bag *out* of your suitcase before sending it through."

Gus wasn't happy with the scolding. *It's not like I have a bag full of chemical explosives in there,* he thought.

But the agent must have thought otherwise.

"We have to keep this mouthwash, sir. It's more than three ounces." And with that, Gus found himself defenseless. Fuming, he surrendered his oversized bottle of mouthwash, stopped quickly at Hudson News to buy more, then darted toward the tram.

Two hours and fifteen minutes later, he landed. Once on the shuttle to his hotel, he was able to sit back and breathe in the smells of a new city. Gus closed his eyes and savored the air, packed with optimism and warm welcome. He was ready to nail down this job. *If the worst thing that happens today is a confiscated bottle of mouthwash, I'm doing pretty well*, he assured himself. He sat back and smiled, relishing the last few minutes of relaxation before his busy day.

At the hotel, Gus didn't waste any time getting dressed for his interviews—four in a row with no downtime in between. He quickly washed up and changed into his suit.

But as he put on his pants, something felt funny. Gus looked in the mirror.

Oh, crap.

Out of haste and in the early morning darkness, he had packed the wrong suit, the one he was hoping would fit him again—someday.

Today, it was two sizes too small.

He couldn't even zip up the trousers, much less hook them at the waist. And his first interview was in thirty minute—no time to get a new suit.

With those limitations, Gus had to think fast. On his way out to the cab, he stopped at the front desk and requested a safety pin. From the back seat of the taxi, he zipped up his fly as far as it would go, which was only halfway, and pinned the rest, his belt concealing the unclosed portion. Hoping to cover his gaffe even further, he buttoned his jacket all the way down.

He wasn't about to lose confidence, though. Knowing his knowledge would speak for itself, he would play up the chemistry. Distract them from what he was wearing.

Gus used his right arm for all the formalities, such as extending his strong handshake, handing over his resume, and holding his fork steady at lunch. He laughed, asked questions, and boasted his accomplishments. He presented his PowerPoint, took notes, and shook more hands.

His right hand dominated the scene that day.

Because for the entire day—and all four interviews—his left hand was stationed permanently over his pinned-up mistake.

The interviewers' reactions? Suffice it to say that Gus was sent home with job offers.

It was the good chemistry, no doubt.

Historic Error

While a teenager, JoAnn bore all the responsibility for her baby brother, which meant she had to forgo all after-school activities with friends and, ultimately, her entire social life. To fill that gap, she immersed herself in characters and events of long ago and far away. She was especially fascinated by Chinese history. Although she had read a great deal about it, she longed for someone to talk to about all those ideologies, dynasties, and alternating periods of political unity and disunity dating back to the beginning of written Chinese history, in 1600 BC.

But alas, her increasingly esoteric vocabulary, consisting of odd-looking words like "feudal," "hegemons," and "eunuchs," was left to simmer, unspoken, in her mind.

So when the petite, ninety-pound college freshman got the chance to audit an upper division course in Chinese history, she seized the opportunity. It was her first week on campus, and autumn had never been more brilliant, with the beds of luscious flowers in their last and most majestic days overlapping the appearance of vivid, yellow leaves on aspens and cottonwoods. JoAnn walked toward the pillared building and stared at her school's name engraved across the top. This was nirvana.

She took a deep breath, entered the building, and climbed the stairs to the lecture hall on the second floor. "Oh college, I love you!" she whispered as she slid into what she hoped would be her usual seat, three rows from the front, and directly in her new professor's line of vision.

The Chinese History prof looked just as she had pictured him: tall, dignified, knowledgeable, animated, and of course, wearing a tweed sport coat. A mere child in the company of upperclassmen, JoAnn exuded uncommon confidence, thanks to the tomes of Chinese history she had devoured over the past few years. She found herself nodding as her professor poured out everything he knew about the Chinese. Nodding showed she was engaged, interested, and a little knowledgeable herself. The fact of the matter was, there was very little he could tell her that she didn't already know. But she wouldn't let on. This was his stage.

On that particular day, the subject of eunuchs came up. JoAnn was familiar with eunuchs from her reading, so she rested her arm on the side of her desk, adjusted her glasses, and placed her pen on her notebook as her instructor embarked on his lecture.

"It was during the Shang Dynasty that eunuchs made their appearance," he said. "Shang kings castrated prisoners of war. It was usually a punishment, but for some eunuchs, agreeing to castration, or even self-castrating, was a means of gaining employment in the Imperial service."

JoAnn nodded, although she wondered why he was pronouncing it "you-nix." She almost didn't catch what he was talking about. And she was a little embarrassed for this distinguished professor, mispronouncing a word so significant in Chinese history. But she was a mere freshman, and an auditor at that, so it wasn't her place to correct the teacher. She continued to nod.

"Many eunuchs were allowed to rise to high ranks," the instructor continued, "because, since they weren't able to have children, eunuchs wouldn't threaten to seize power and start a competing dynasty."

JoAnn continued to nod, but this was getting distracting. *I think he needs to know he's not saying that word right.*

"By 1912, there were only 450 Imperial eunuchs left, as the Chinese stopped this practice. And today, there's only a handful of Imperial eunuchs still alive as far as we know."

Well, if I don't tell him, he's going to embarrass himself year after year.

Her hand shot up. The professor nodded to her.

JoAnn slipped off her glasses and held them in her hand to look authoritative. "Uh, I believe that word is pronounced 'unch,'" said the well-read college freshman.

Dead silence. Then snickers and twitters undulated across the lecture hall like a "wave" at a football game.

"Uh, no, it is not," replied the professor.

She could say nothing. Shamed into silence, JoAnn looked down at her notebook and pretended to take notes, twisting her hair with her pinky.

Campus life was not quite as ideal after that. To avoid the "Unch Girl" taunts whispered behind her back on more than one occasion, she moved permanently to the last row, off to the right. She kept a dictionary at her side and learned to flip the pages discreetly to check the pronunciation of words before she spoke.

And JoAnn never corrected a professor again.

Well, maybe in her mind, but certainly not out loud.

Dance at Zero Dark Thirty

S ummer 1986.
Jacksonville, North Carolina. Camp Johnson.
United States Marine Corps Admin School.

Lance Corporal Amos snarled at the darkness that engulfed him in the barracks that morning. As was the case from time to time, he'd been placed in charge of marching the formation to the mess hall. This was no ragtag platoon from *M*A*S*H*—these were the United States Marines, the seaborne infantry arm of the U.S. war machine, a group of some of the best and toughest fighters in the world.

And Lance Corporal Amos had the daunting task of marching them to breakfast. Daunting because, shy and only nineteen, he outranked his fellow trainees, many of whom were older but so low in rank that they were called "non-rates." Daunting also because he had no real training addressing a large formation at a bellow and commanding them to perform precise drill commands. Daunting because there was a brain-load to remember in marching a formation, not unlike choreographing a line dance. And the stakes were high: Marines could trip. Marines could stumble. Without the requisite precision, this Marine Corps unit could come across as *not* the best and toughest fighters in the world.

This was the responsibility Lance Corporal Amos bore that morning at four o'clock.

As he readied himself for roll call, he reviewed the route from the barracks to the chow hall. It had two turns: a right, and then a left. He mentally practiced his calls. It would be important for the cadence of the turn commands—"Column left, MARCH! Column right, MARCH!"—to fall on a particular foot in order to successfully change the direction of the formation.

Okay, he thought. *If you're turning left, your right foot needs to be forward, otherwise you cross your legs when you turn. That means the "march" needs to come on the left foot, then you take one more step and turn. Working backward from that, you need to start the phrase "column left" on the right foot, to make sure the "march" comes at the correct point in the cadence.*

Complex thinking for zero dark thirty.

But now, with reveille ending, Lance Corporal Amos felt ready. He took a deep breath. More than one hundred marines, four deep, were assembled in front of the barracks that morning. The best and toughest fighters in the world.

Off they marched to the ostensibly confident commands of their leader.

As the formation approached the right turn, Lance Corporal Amos was so busy thinking about the cadence and which foot to start on that he called, "Column left, MARCH!"

Oops, he meant column right.

Two of the lead marines followed the instruction as given, as they were trained to do. And off they went on their left turn—right into a ditch.

The other two lead marines, perhaps better fortified with the gift of common sense—they were, after all, graduates of any of the numerous USMC schools—recognized the error, skipped a step, and turned right.

Those who immediately followed were forced to dance, and turned either left or right, as they could, in an impressive display of boogie walking, ankle rocking, and . . . was someone doing the Electric Slide over there?

With legs flying in all directions, the entire formation quickly disintegrated.

Lance Corporal Amos thereafter enjoyed his rank of "that guy who crashed the chow formation."

At least he wasn't a non-rate.